ASK about the...

Academic's Support Kit

The **Academic's Support Kit** is a unique resource that provides all the information, skills and guidance to support academic professional development.

The **Kit** offers a wealth of references, techniques and practical advice in the following 6 books:

- Building Your Academic Career
- Getting Started in Research
- Writing for Publication
- Teaching and Supervision
- Winning and Managing Research Funding
- Building Networks

The **Kit** comes in a durable, plastic slip case for easy storage.

This taster includes sample chapters from each of the books in the **Kit** - we hope you enjoy reading these.

To order your copy at a **special price of £79** (usual price £99) **valid until 1 February 2005** please call SAGE Customer Service on 020 7324 8703 or buy online at www.sagepub.co.uk

Academic's Support Kit
December 2004 * 808 pages
ISBN 0-7619-4232-7

If you require any further information about the **Kit** please e-mail the marketing manager at SAGE Publications:
janey.walker@sagepub.co.uk

ASK about the...

Authors

Rebecca Boden, from England, is professor of accounting at the University of the West of England. She did her PhD in politics immediately after graduating from her first degree (which was in history and politics). She worked as a contract researcher in a university before the shortage of academic jobs in 1980s Britain forced her into the Civil Service as a tax inspector. She subsequently launched herself on to the unsuspecting world of business schools as an accounting academic.

Debbie Epstein, a South African, is professor in the School of Social Sciences at Cardiff University. She did her first degree in history and then worked briefly as a research assistant on the philosopher Jeremy Bentham's papers. However, unable to read his handwriting, she went on to teach children in a variety of schools for seventeen years. She returned to university to start her PhD in her forties and has been an academic ever since.

Jane Kenway, an Australian, is professor of education at Monash University with particular responsibility for developing the field of global cultural studies in education. She was a schoolteacher and outrageous hedonist before she became an academic. But since becoming an academic she has also become a workaholic, which has done wonders for her social life, because, fortunately, all her friends are similarly inclined. Nonetheless she is interested in helping next generation academics to be differently pleasured with regard to their work and their lives.

Contents

SAGE Publications Ltd
1 Oliver's Yard
55 City Road
London EC1Y 1SP

SAGE Publications Inc.
2455 Teller Road
Thousand Oaks, California 91320

SAGE Publications India Pvt Ltd
B-42, Panchsheel Enclave
Post Box 4109
New Delhi 110 017

Typeset by C&M Digitals (P) Ltd, Chennai, India
Printed in Great Britain by Athenaeum Press Ltd., Gateshead, Tyne & Wear

6   Balancing Acts: between Work and Life

In this chapter we try to convince you to have a life outside work. This is one instance in which we are not writing from the basis of our own personal expertise and experience. All three of us are hopeless workaholics with a poor work–life balance. However, as Jane said in introducing herself at the beginning of the book, we would like to help the next generation of academics to be differently pleasured. So do as we say, not as we do.

What do we mean, 'work–life balance'?

This much used phrase is a euphemism for something much more simple and straightforward: how much time you spend working or not working and how the quality of your non-working time is affected by your work practices.

People with a poor work–life balance (that is, people who work too hard and for too long) end up with broken relationships, disrupted family lives, physical and mental health problems and poor quality of life. No job is worth this. Research in the UK and elsewhere indicates that academics are much more likely to become seriously ill with workplace stress than a whole range of supposedly more stressful professional occupations. We are sure that this pattern would be replicated in many, if not all, countries in the world. The same group of workers are also renowned for the punishing length of their working week.

Don't think you are immune from all this. Take positive steps now to redress the balance in your life and keep it that way.

Why do academics work too long?

Academic work has a number of inherent characteristics that produce a tendency to excessive and prolonged periods of intensive labour. First, the work itself and the standard that is expected are generally very poorly defined. When combined with a culture of competitive critique, this means that enough is never enough. Second, much academic work is subject to what Jane has called 'discourses of derision' in another context. That is, especially outside the 'hard' sciences, academic work can all too often be seen as of little or no value in a system where increasing emphasis is placed on the production of 'useful' knowledge. This derision often finds fertile ground among academics themselves, who either suffer from low self-esteem combined with compulsive over-achievement, or find it hard to see why anyone should pay them a salary to pursue the things they're interested in (or both). Third, academic work is frequently invisible, and tangible outputs such as publications give little indication of the actual value of the labour taken to produce them. Together, these characteristics serve to create a view of academic work, frequently internalised by academics themselves, that casts it as self-indulgent, useless and marked by long periods of time-wasting inactivity.

This poor understanding and perception of much academic work means that there is very little defence against pressure to do more and more and more and to do it better and quicker. When people protest or fall ill, the institutional response is all too frequently to place the problem firmly at the door of the individual. Thus people who cannot cope are deemed to be poor self-managers or time managers. University systems are marked by an abject lack of reflexivity in this regard.

Discourses of time management

We have already indicated the first discourse of time management and the one most often deployed against academics and, unfortunately, inhabited by them. This is the discourse of wasted time, poor self-organisation and lack of professionalism. In this discourse, academics are useless wastrels who simply don't know what a hard day's work is and spend way too much time doing nothing or watching daytime television. If you are not managing to keep up with your work, then it's entirely down to you and your inadequacies.

The second discourse of time management, and one that we would like to promote and inhabit, is one in which time is recognised as being in short supply but in which we can take a certain degree of control and do something to ameliorate things.

There is a really fine line between these two discourses and it's treacherously easy to slip from one into the other in the twinkling of an eye. There is also a fine line between occupying the second discourse in a positive way and it being a way of not participating or being a good colleague. If you slip into the latter position, the second discourse can easily become an expression of bitter, negative sentiments and resentments. You need to understand that care and regard for yourself is not necessarily negative selfishness. Most people struggle with these balances and virtually none of us gets them right all the time.

We offer below some final handy hints (to ourselves as well as to you) on having a good work–life balance and staying sane. It is our New Year's Resolution to follow all of them, and, if we don't manage it, not to criticise ourselves too much for our failures.

Handy hints for maintaining a good work–life balance

1. Build work-free space and activities into your daily routines. These can range from going for a nice walk with your dog, having dinner with your partner, going to the gym or the swimming pool, spending time in your garden, reading a newspaper or a novel, playing computer games or whatever pleases and relaxes you. Don't ever be guilt-tripped into thinking that you can do such things only as rewards or treats for having done your work.
2. Place strict limits on your periods of work. You may have to relax them from time to time in order to meet important deadlines, but in the main you should keep to them and take time off in lieu if you break them. Always try to have at least one work-free day during a normal working week and preferably two. Remember, even God rested on the seventh day.
3. Most academics do at least some of their work at home. Whilst this can be quite nice it can also make it quite difficult to switch off from work activities. If you have the space, make sure that your work-at-home activities are confined to a comfortable and discrete space. About the last thing you need is your computer winking at you as

you try to sleep, eat your dinner or watch television. If you can't afford this luxury then at least try to put your work away, cover your computer up and get on with the rest of your life at the end of your working day/week.

4. Try to organise your working time so that you can use it as efficiently as possible. For instance, make time for complex, demanding tasks in joined-up chunks rather than odd little bits. That way, you have more chance of achieving something and feeling able to have your day(s) of rest.

5. Given the impossibility of academic work-loads and your new resolve to have a good work–life balance, there will inevitably be things at work that you will simply not have time to do. You should be the person who decides what you are going to do and what you are going to leave undone. Your decision should be based solely on your professional judgement about what you need to do to be a good researcher and a good teacher. If you have to make the choice between completing an important research paper or filling in a form that will simply be filed and forgotten, it is obvious to us, and hopefully to you, which choice you should make.

6. When you are working, don't work so hard that you are left too exhausted and depleted to enjoy your non-working time. In the same vein, make sure that your working space (at home and in your office) is safe. Do not put up with non-ergonomic furniture that is likely to compromise your health in any way. It's no good having a good work–life balance if work has left you too unwell to enjoy the rest of your life.

7. Use at least some of your non-working time in a productive, enjoyable and creative way to look after yourself and your health. For instance, being an academic can be a very sedentary occupation, so getting a moderate amount of exercise can be an important and profitable way of spending your leisure time. But don't let this become a punishment either. If you are someone who needs time just to veg out, then take it.

8. We think that getting away from everything from time to time is a wonderful therapy. Do take proper holidays, even if it's just visiting friends and family rather than more expensive trips. Do not take your work with you. If necessary, get someone else to check your suitcase before you leave, if you are completely untrustworthy in

that regard. A complete break, even if it is short, is likely to be much more therapeutic than simply slacking off for a few days.

9. You need to enlist the support of your friends, family and partner in achieving a good work–life balance. Debbie often initially resents it when her partner insists that she has a day off from work. By the end of the day, however, she is grateful for this stiffening of her resolve. It's often the case that academics have other academics as partners and/or friends – after all, who else would put up with you? In one sense this can be quite helpful, as you have people around you who understand precisely what the pressures of your job are. In another sense, it can be quite problematic if you collude together to maintain a poor work–life balance. Whoever or whatever your friends/family are, you need to resolve how you will manage this issue.

And finally ...

This book has been about the various elements of an academic career, how you get the right mix of activities for you, get the jobs you want and how you can balance your work with the rest of life. Throughout, we have emphasised that, although you are part of a massive globalised system, you do have agency over your life and work and can make real choices.

Anne Gold, an academic at the University of London, has devised an exercise for academics designed to help them balance all the aspects of their work and the rest of their life. We think it might be good for you to do an adapted version of her exercise on your own or with friends. You'll need a very large sheet of paper (flip-chart paper is good) and some coloured pens.

Draw a series of buckets. Four of them should be labelled 'research', 'teaching', 'administration' and 'consultancy and practitioner work' in turn. These are your work buckets. In addition, draw the other buckets that best represent your desired life outside work. These might be labelled 'family responsibilities', 'leisure', 'friends', 'relationships', 'health', 'personal and household care and management' and so on. You decide.

In each of the buckets, draw a contents level indicating how full it is – anything from empty to overflowing. Then sit and think about whether you're happy with this distribution and what redistributions are both desirable to, and achievable for you. Address each bucket in turn, consider whether its contents are appropriate and think about strategies for emptying it or filling it up. That is, how are you going to redistribute your energies and efforts? It may be that the total volume of stuff in your buckets is too great. If so, draw one final extra-large bucket to put your unwanted surplus in. Label it the 'phucket bucket'.

3   The Research Process

If you've started to formulate research questions, you have gone a good way towards beginning a research project. The next stage is to write a plan of your intended work to act as a guide and to make sure that you think through the major issues before you begin. In this chapter we will guide you through the process of writing research plans, or proposals, stage by stage. At each stage, we detail what you need to think about.

What is a research proposal?

Once you know what you want do your research about and have formulated some research questions, you need to think about how you will actually carry out the research. Doing a research project always involves several different activities and sorts of thinking, some sequential, some running in parallel and some iterative.

Because research is a complex process, it's always a good idea to write yourself a good plan of where you are going and what you are going to do along the way. In this way, you will have a kind of route map to guide you as you travel the research path. However, this path is a little like the roads in *Alice through the Looking Glass*: it sometimes changes direction when you are not looking. So it's important to remember that you can't rely on the map completely. You must keep revisiting it and adjusting it to your changing needs and directions.

These route maps are usually called research proposals. There are some situations in which you may well be required to write a research proposal. For example:

- If you want a place on a research degree programme.
- If you want a bursary to do a research degree.
- In some universities it will form part of a progression exam on a research degree programme.

- If you are looking for funding for your research, however small, from your own university or some external funding body.
- In some cases, especially when the research is in collaboration with or investigating an external body, that body will need to see the proposal in order to decide whether or not to give you access and assistance to do your research.
- If you want your employer to give you time to do the research; for example, you may want a reduced teaching load or a sabbatical or paid time off from a non-university job to allow you to do the research.
- You may need to get formal approval from your university that your proposed research conforms to certain ethical guidelines. In order to gain this approval, you will need to present a proposal.

In any case, even if you are not required to write a research proposal, it's a really good idea to do one for your own benefit. Writing a research proposal will:

- Help you to be sure that you have a viable research project.
- Provide a clear 'route map' for the research.
- Enable you to identify any possible problems and issues with the proposed project.
- Assist you in choosing an appropriate supervisor or mentor who knows the area in which you are interested. (More on choosing mentors later.)
- Help your mentor or supervisor support you, as they will know what it is you are trying to do.
- Give a project a momentum of its own, almost a material form.
- Give you a reference point to monitor your progress as the project develops. This can give you a lot of confidence and a big boost to your morale.

Writing research proposals

What we will do now is take you through the generic stages and sections of a research proposal. Whatever your discipline or research area, you will need to give consideration to the matters we are about to describe. However, the language you use to address these may differ according to your disciplinary home, as will the relative weightings you give to the various aspects. Also, your proposal will need to be tailored to the specific expectations of its various audiences, such as research funding bodies, PhD committees and so on. This is discussed further in *Winning and Managing Research Funding*. For your own purposes, your research proposal is likely to include a section on each of the following areas:

- Background and rationale: the 'so what?' -ness of the research topic.
- Research questions: what, precisely, are you trying to find out?
- Available literature: the public story so far.
- Theoretical frameworks: the e-word and the o-word.
- Methods: your investigative and analytical techniques.
- Ethical considerations: will your research do harm?
- Time scales: establishing phases and deadlines.
- Dissemination: getting it out and about.

Writing your proposal will be an iterative process, especially in relation to your reading and framing of questions, but remember that, like a lot of academic writing, proposals tend to read best if they are presented in a linear way. The order in which we have outlined the sections is not the only logical order possible and you will have to decide what works for your proposal, always remembering that what you present must be clear, coherent and cogent. Remember, also, that in an actual research process the various stages of research run concurrently, iteratively and sequentially.

Background and rationale: the 'so what?' -ness of the research topic

Now is the time to go back to your hardback notebook, as the notes that you made on your research topic and the 'so what?' -ness of it are about to come into their own.

This section needs to explain the background, issues and the 'so what?' -ness of your proposed research. As we explained before, the best research issues usually start because someone has been curious about the world immediately around them or has had their interest stimulated by something they have seen, heard or read. You might care to start with your own experiences, describing how it is that you came to be interested in the subject – a brief 'autobiography of the question'.

The importance or 'so what?' -ness of the proposed research will lie in the contribution you think it can make to knowledge, to intellectual and theoretical debates, to policy and practice in particular areas – in sum, to our understanding of the world. You need to use this section to convince the readers of the proposal (and yourself) that your project is worth the time and trouble.

Research questions: what, precisely, are you trying to find out?

It is essential to formulate your research questions very clearly and explicitly in your proposal. If you have more than one principal question, you may want to number them. If you have subsidiary questions, they should come immediately after the principal question they relate to. It is necessary to have an answerable question that is clear and sufficiently well defined/focused for you to do the research implied within an appropriate time-frame and the available resources.

If you work in an area in which you are required to put your questions in the form of formal hypotheses, these need to be very clearly stated and numbered. The usual convention is to number them as H_1, H_2, H_3 and so on.

Available literature: the public story so far

In developing your research topic and questions you will already have engaged with the literature sufficiently to be able to give a good account of what is known about the answers to your questions and which theories and concepts you expect to find particularly useful. The proposal itself will contain only a relatively short section on the existing literature, but what you write there will need to demonstrate that you know what you are doing and have a good idea of what has been done before.

To reiterate, this is *not* the same as reviewing the literature to find a gap, which, as we explained above, is a bit of a trap for unwary researchers. You will already have a fairly clear idea of what sort of thing you want to look at and therefore your visit to the literature isn't to find a topic. Rather, the proposal needs to make two points clear on the subject of literature.

- First, you need to talk about the work of others that provides empirical data and/or creative insights that contribute to answering your questions. This will demonstrate that you have refined your questions, and that the answers you eventually produce are likely be a real contribution to knowledge. You will be able to show what further evidence you need to collect to answer your research questions more fully.
- Second, reference to the literature will enable you to pinpoint those theories and concepts useful to you in trying to make sense of your own research.

Most important, you must make a convincing case as to why your research would create valuable and useful knowledge that builds upon or challenges existing work in the field.

Theoretical frameworks: the e-word and the o-word

One of the problems we frequently see in research proposals is the absence of any explicit theoretical framework. Research without a theoretical framework is description and does not qualify as academic research or as a contribution to knowledge. We cannot say it too often or too loudly.

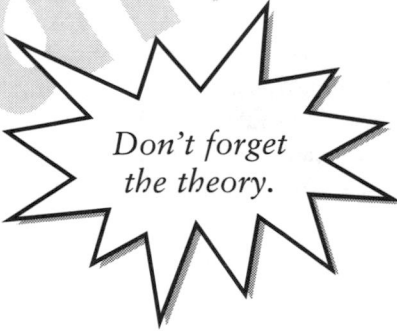

Don't forget the theory.

One of the biggest reasons why people avoid talking or writing about theory is that they feel excluded by the language which people use. In particular, it may take a long time to be confident in the use of commonly used words in academic writing (but not in the rest of the world) such as 'epistemology' and 'ontology'.

Debbie, Rebecca and Jane all admit, to each other and now to you, that when they were novice researchers they had to return to the dictionary many times to clarify their understanding of 'epistemology' and 'ontology'. Here is our best attempt to explain them in readily understandable ways.

Epistemology

Here's one of the many dictionary definitions that we find useful:

'The philosophical theory of knowledge, which seeks to define it, distinguish its principal varieties, identify its sources, and establish its limits'

(from *The New Fontana Dictionary of Modern Thought*)

What this means to us is that epistemology is a theoretical framework for making sense of how the world works or some aspect of how the world works. It's about what counts as knowledge in your world view. For example, all three of us are feminists and we see feminism as an epistemology. What this means, in practice, is that the lens through which we view the world is shaped by certain understandings about gender, power and the position of women. So an epistemology may be defined as a particular sort of lens that allows you to make sense of some aspect of the world around you in a particular way. Different lenses (different epistemologies) will obviously give different views. No epistemology can give you a total view of the world, because they only allow you to see from particular perspectives. So it's useful to have a whole range of epistemologies available. Foucault conceptualised this as a theory toolbox.

Everybody, in daily life, no matter what they do, makes sense of the world according to their understandings and theories about it. These may take the form of religious beliefs or common sense or cultural values or social norms and they may not be explicit or apparent even to the person themselves. What distinguishes academic research epistemologies from these everyday epistemologies is that they are expected to be explicit, rigorously defined and robust. That is why we call them theories. You cannot make sense of your data without an epistemology/theory.

▶ *Ontology*

If 'epistemology' is about what counts as knowledge, 'ontology' is concerned with the nature of the knower. It is about how our place in the world, identity and embodied experiences impact on the way in which we see the world and, consequentially, the epistemologies that we find meaningful and useful. It follows that our ontological perspective will have a significant impact on which epistemologies we are drawn to and how we use them. We've noticed that the early authors in new fields of enquiry such as gender, race, sexuality and disability are often ontologically steeped in the issues they are investigating: they are women, ethnic minority people, lesbian or gay people, or people with mental or physical impairments.

In your 'autobiography of the question' you will have begun, either implicitly or possibly explicitly, to make connections between your own ontology and epistemology.

We do not believe that any knowledge is 'objective' or that researchers can take a god-like stance as knowers. It is therefore important to be clear, up-front and honest about your ontology and epistemology in your research. This will enable your readers to understand where you are coming from and to make a judgement on the quality of your work based on that understanding. Saying who you are and where you are coming from will not stop people who genuinely believe in the possibility of 'objective truth' from criticising you for being partial and subjective. But at least, in contrast to them, you will have been honest about your subjectivity and partiality. And remember, subjectivity is not and should never be synonymous with lack of rigour. Being clear about your frameworks is part of that rigour.

You should therefore use your proposal to clarify what theoretical resources you will be drawing on and why. There should, therefore, be clear linkages between this discussion and your discussion of the literature. In particular, you need to explain the relevance and usefulness of your theoretical framework to your proposed project. You need to give particular consideration, at this point, to the issues that loom large within your chosen theoretical framework and how they will affect the research process.

Methodology and methods: your investigative and analytical techniques

Definitions of methodology differ confusingly and vary greatly between disciplines. However, a reasonable definition is that it is the package of epistemology, ontology and method that shapes and informs your research project. People in different disciplines have different methodological approaches:

Methods are the ways in which you go about collecting, locating or creating the material you are going to analyse and the associated practical techniques. For example:

- A cultural theorist might use auto/biography, stories and myths, novels, poetry and plays, visual images, films and television programmes, newspapers and so on.
- People in the creative arts often produce a work of art, a play or an exhibition and write an exegesis of it.
- An art historian might use both cultural artefacts and archival material about the people who created and consumed them.
- An economist might garner government statistical data and use this to construct a model to generate research results.
- A sociologist might go out and interview people, participate in some aspect of their lives or distribute survey questionnaires.

It's difficult to find a collective name for all the different kinds of material mentioned here. In the social sciences, it tends to be called 'data' and, for convenience, we will use this term. But remember that we are using the term inclusively.

Finally, there are research traditions that don't rely on data, even as broadly defined. These are the types of research – such as pure mathematics, logic and some branches of philosophy and theology – which are purely conceptual and directed at the resolution of abstract problems.

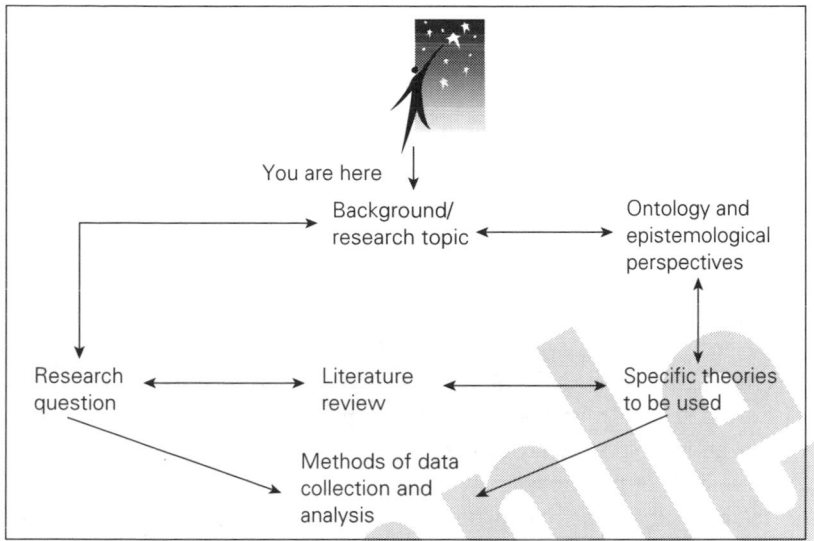

FIGURE 3   Processes and linkages in research proposals

We've already explained that the proposal mirrors the research process itself and therefore, like research, your proposal must represent a coherent and integrated process. The questions you are seeking to address, together with your epistemological perspectives, will inform the methods you choose. The methods you decide to use should enable you collect and analyse the data that you need in order to answer your questions using your chosen epistemological perspectives. Figure 3 gives a visual image of the kinds of processes and linkages discussed so far that should be explicit in your proposal.

To summarise, this section of a research proposal should consist of a detailed description and justification of how you will actually go about collecting and analysing your data. That is, what data will you collect, how will you collect it and how will it be analysed? You need to justify why these are the best methods for your question(s).

Use your imagination in solving the problem of how to collect the data that you need. People often resort to what seems like the simplest, easiest and even the most 'objective' method of data collection. This is not necessarily the best method for answering the questions you are trying to ask. Methods such as questionnaires, for example, may evoke feelings of fatigue and *ennui* among the target recipients, especially if those recipients have no empathy with, or particular interest in, what you are researching. On the other hand, where people feel strongly about an issue a questionnaire may be a very good source of data. At Rebecca's university, for example, a long and detailed questionnaire survey to all staff about the research culture in the institution produced a very healthy and very rapid response rate. Rebecca attributes this to the fact that staff were either antithetical to research or deeply committed to it. Either way, everyone was very keen to have their say.

Helen and James demonstrated admirable ingenuity and imagination in designing their data collection methods.

Helen, a marketing academic, was researching people's food shopping and consumption habits. She needed to know what they bought and how they used it. Rather than simply send out a questionnaire or carry out an interview based on memory, she asked her respondents to write a list of the foodstuffs in their fridges and cupboards. She used the list as the basis of a guided discussion with the respondents.

James was doing research in cultural studies/sociology on how children form their identities, including how they see 'home' and the part it plays in who they think they are. As a starting point, he gave the children a disposable camera and asked them to take photographs of 'home' (that is, whatever 'home' meant to them). When he had developed the photographs (including several of front doors and pets) he used them to discuss with the children why those particular images meant 'home' to them.

Practical matters such as whether or not you will get physical access to the data you need or whether you have the practical skills you need to access it are real considerations in research design. Will you have enough time to collect the data required? Will your data collection requirements stretch the goodwill of those on whom you depend for access?

In 1945 the border between Germany and Poland was redrawn and some formerly German territory became part of Poland. As a result, many of the regional government records relating to the formerly German territories passed into Polish archives and were often catalogued in Polish. Cathy

▶

▶ was a fluent German-speaker but her Polish was non-existent. Access to these crucial records was therefore dependent not only on obtaining funding for research trips to Poland, but also on learning enough Polish to interrogate the catalogues and negotiate with Polish archivists.

In this section, it is absolutely essential to describe not only how you will collect your data but also how you will analyse it. Data analysis is often scantily done or left out completely. This seriously weakens many proposals.

Data analysis needs two things: first, an appropriate theoretical lens through which to view and make sense of the material collected; second, appropriate tools and techniques to organise, categorise, sift and manage it. You will need to refer back to your theoretical framework and your research questions to be absolutely sure that you explain how you will use and address them in your analysis of your data.

Explain what skills you will need and whether you have them or how you will acquire them. Think about the particular software or other tools available (see later in this book), and how you will acquire the skills to use them. It's a good idea to visualise yourself sitting down with your carefully collected data and asking 'What do I do now? How do I make sense of all of this?'

Ethical considerations: will your research do harm?

Later in this book we will give detailed consideration to ethical practice in research. For the proposal, you will need to ensure that your reader is confident that you have thought carefully about the ethical dimensions of your proposed research and, where appropriate, that you intend to comply with all relevant ethical guidelines and procedures. Sometimes research may have no obvious ethical issues attached to it. However, we think that research completely devoid of any ethical considerations or consequences whatsoever is a virtual impossibility.

Time scales: establishing phases and deadlines

It is important to map out a reasonable schedule of your work so that you can monitor your progress and manage your project effectively. If your project is externally funded, bear in mind that your funders may also ask for a time schedule and even ask you to report against it. Start with your intended finishing date and do not underestimate the amount of time that it takes to polish your draft writing into a finished product.

In Table 3, we show the timeline of a real project involving a number of researchers. On this project the researchers had to juggle a number of conflicting time constraints. These included the time scale that the organisation under investigation imposed, the need to use research assistants and also the proposers' own busy schedules. Note that many of the activities are concurrent.

Making an impact: getting it out and about

You need to make a clear statement in your proposal about how you intend your work to have an impact. We deal with this issue in much more detail in *Building Networks*. Making an impact may involve three different sorts of dissemination of your research output.

To other academics

A key indicator of the worth of much research is whether it is publishable in refereed academic journals, as an academic book or as a chapter in an academic book. You may like to give some consideration at this stage to what sorts of things may be publishable and where you would like them to appear.

Also think about which conferences you may wish to give papers at. This may involve conferences that will give you high academic visibility, which can help with your career prospects, but just as important is to find smaller conferences where you can have a good and detailed discussion about your work and get constructive feedback that will help you improve your papers and other writing. If you are seeking funding for your project, you may be able to ask for money to go to these conferences as part of the research funds.

This kind of dissemination is especially important if you wish to pursue a career as an academic in a university.

To relevant non-academic users and beneficiaries of your research

These may include people who were involved in the research process as gatekeepers and/or respondents, possibly the people who funded your

TABLE 3 Women's participation in research activities

Date	Task	Responsibilities
2002 May	Advertise researcher posts internally Submission of proposal and consent procedures to university ethics committee	PMG
25 June	Interviews for researcher posts	
1 September	Project starts	RA
September–December	Initial literature review (reading of the literature continues throughout the project)	RA
September–December	Analysis of secondary data on women in science	RA
September–October	Design of research instruments	RA, PMG
October	Advisory group meeting to advise on research design and access	
End October	Submission of survey questionnaire and interview schedule to ethics committee	RA, PMG
November	Distribution of survey questionnaire	RA
December–Early January 2003	Survey data entry	Casual employee(s)
December–January 2003	Interview recruitment	RA
January	Survey data analysis	RA, PMG
February–June	Interviews	RA
May–July	Interview data analysis	RA, PMG
July–September	Preparation of report	RA, PMG
September	Draft report to advisory group	PMG
October	Dissemination of report Seminar to present findings	RA, PMG
2003–4	Conference attendance Preparation/submission of papers for publication	RA, PMG

PMG Project Management Group. *RA* Research Associate.

research and, indeed, anyone else or any other groups who might find your work of use or interest.

The form of such dissemination may include a workshop for policy users, articles in appropriate professional journals or newspapers, a popular book, magazine articles or public lectures. For instance, if you were conducting research into children and young people, you might want to hold a special conference for such groups of people and include it in the costings and dissemination strategy.

Through the popular media

This means of dissemination can reach wider audiences and, if well done, can be effective and very beneficial to your personal research profile and that of your university. However, media exposure is fraught with dangers and we would strongly advise you to seek professional help, support and training in how to deal with journalists. Your institution's press office should be able to help in this regard. A good way of attracting media attention is by producing good press releases. Again, your institution's press office, if there is one, should be able to guide you in this. If you anticipate that your research will attract media interest, make sure that there are plans for dealing with it in your proposal, especially if that interest is likely to be hostile.

And finally ...

When you have done all this and have a complete draft research proposal, get other people, your peers as well as those more experienced than you, to read it and comment. This will help you to revise the proposal before you proceed further. That way, you will ensure that you start off on a firm footing.

4   Publishing Articles in Academic Journals

Having covered the basics, we turn our attention in this chapter to some of the complexities and details of how to write journal articles and get them published in refereed academic journals.

What do we mean, 'academic journals'?

We find that undergraduate students often get confused about the difference between academic literature and other sorts of publication when doing literature reviews. This is often because we haven't been specific enough about what we mean by 'academic journals'. What we do mean are publications, on paper or electronic, which contain scholarly articles that present some or all of the following: research findings, new knowledge, new theorisations or interesting syntheses or re-presentations of existing knowledge. The authors and the readers are usually academics, but not necessarily so.

Academic journals are, therefore, the 'chat rooms' for the exchange of knowledge and ideas and for debate. In fact, this is exactly the reason why the scientific community invented academic journals in the eighteenth century. They were, and remain, an important mechanism by which geographically disparate scholars can communicate and share their thinking.

Journals have a particular structure. They are always edited by one or more academics, who take overall responsibility for the shape and character of the journal. They generally also have editorial boards, usually drawn from the international academic community and chosen to reflect the range of interests of the journal. They may be more or less actively engaged in the processes of publishing the journal. Journals come out regularly, usually three or four times a year, and from time to time may have special issues edited by guest editors on particular themes. In most cases, however, each edition of the journal will present a fairly eclectic mix of papers, but all within the broad remit of the particular journal.

Another common misconception, but this time more often among postgraduate students and less experienced faculty, is that articles in professional journals are on a par, in research terms, with refereed papers in academic journals. Be in no doubt about this, among academics, academic journals are much more prestigious. But of course, writing for appropriate professional audiences is a means of achieving good dissemination of your work to those who might use it in theirs is important.

Some people think that writing for professional audiences is a good apprenticeship for doing academic writing. Indeed, early publication in professional journals can boost people's confidence, stimulate access to research fields and also help people experience the personal satisfaction of getting into print. But, these benefits are sometimes all too elusive and outweighed by two very serious risks.

First, the two genres are quite distinct, albeit related, forms. Professional journal articles based on academic research are really translations of academic writing for lay readerships. That is, they represent an attempt to render academic work more accessible to a wider audience. Logically, therefore, it is not possible to write for professional audiences before the academic thinking and writing have been done. Further, given that the genres are quite different, the writing skills you need to write for one do not necessarily translate into writing for the other.

Second, some inexperienced academics spend so much time and effort on writing for practitioners that they never engage with academic audiences, convincing themselves that they have done the academic job when really they haven't. A further problem for such people is that the quality of their writing for professionals is frequently rather poor because it is not grounded in the rigorous thinking and peer review processes that academic journals demand and provide. In short, putting the professional before the academic means that this stuff simply doesn't go through the academic mill and is therefore unrefined and unimproved.

> Jennifer had established herself as a successful writer for the technical, professional press prior to commencing her research career. For these audiences, and for editors who paid by word length, she had developed a style that was very terse and directly factual. When she started her PhD, it took a long time for her to adapt her writing style to the more discursive, carefully argued approaches that are needed in academic writing.

Why publish in academic journals?

As an academic, you will probably have been subject to quite strong pressure from your institution to publish in academic journals, often because more publications mean more external funding for the university. Pressure to publish may also come from competition for internal promotion. However much universities say officially that they promote people for their teaching excellence, this is often patently untrue. Teaching is virtually always a secondary consideration when committees think about whether someone should be promoted or not. Whilst these pressures to publish are very real and often quite painful, we believe that you should not lose sight of the many much more positive reasons for doing such work.

- Publishing is academic journals is usually an immensely personally rewarding activity that can offer you a sense of progress, 'closure' as you finish one phase of your research, achievement and pride in yourself and your work.
- If you don't publish your work in academic forums you are failing to engage in wider academic debates or add to the body of publicly available knowledge in your field – which is one of the primary purposes of undertaking research in the first place. Remember that reading other people's refereed work helps academics to develop their own thinking, research and teaching.
- The rigorous review processes that your work will undergo will give it a certain standing or 'quality mark'. It is rare for papers to emerge from the review process unimproved – even if bruised authors are sometimes reluctant to admit it. Readers are likely to trust something that is as well written as it can be and which they know has been subject to scrutiny.

This is especially the case if you are trying to influence non-academic readers who might use or engage with your research.

- Quite simply, publishing helps you to build your reputation and that of your research and field. This may be crucial to getting new jobs or promotion.
- If you make a contribution to the research income of your department and/or university by achieving a good publication record, you will indirectly benefit by being a member of a more conducive and better-funded research environment.
- A good publication record will also help when it comes to winning external research funding by making you look more credible. We deal with this subject in *Winning and Managing Research Funding*.

What can I publish?

The first key consideration in deciding whether to publish or not is whether you have anything worthwhile to say at this point. Premature publication is frustrating, messy and really to be avoided. Therefore do not waste your energies and efforts and those of journal editors and peer reviewers or try the patience of readers. Conversely, don't be so coy about your writing that you constantly delay submitting anything for publication because it isn't yet 'perfect'. Perfection is a chimera – it can't be achieved and you can waste a lot of time and energy seeking the holy grail of the Perfect Publishable Paper.

Here is a list of the sorts of papers that you might be interested in writing for publication:

- A paper describing and analysing your empirical or archival data from a research project. This can be written at various stages in the research process – you don't have to wait until the project is completed to write about it. Often researchers find it useful to publish 'along the way' once they have appropriate data to comment on. Of course, you should publish articles (and/or books) on completed research projects too.
- Most journals have special issues around particular themes from time to time. The themes are generally broad and, with imagination, you may be able to craft your research into a paper that fits them.

- A review essay, which takes a critical look at a range of literature in your field, synthesising it and building on it to develop new insights. This can be a good one if you are doing a doctorate and therefore having to really master a whole field of literature.
- A 'think piece' which develops theoretical insights and ideas within your field of enquiry.
- A response to someone else's work. You are more likely to do this when you disagree with someone, but sometimes journals invite specific individuals to respond to a particular piece of work.
- A methodological reflection in which you explore problems and dilemmas that may have arisen in the course of your research. Some fields give rise to much more of this kind of writing than others.
- Some journals have slots for shorter, less developed 'work in progress' reports. These may include a fairly straightforward description of an on-going research project. They can be a good way of getting into print when you are relatively inexperienced or anxious to get a major project 'on the map'.
- Other journals invite 'opinion pieces' about issues that are of current importance. These, too, tend to be shorter than the journal's regular articles and may be more polemic in style.
- Some canny people planning their doctoral theses do so in such a way that they can develop papers for publication in parallel with their dissertation chapters. In this way, they give themselves confidence that their work passes muster; polish, through the refereeing process; and a significant career advantage when they start applying for jobs.

Keep in mind, though, that some of the sorts of pieces listed above may not be peer-reviewed. Whilst you will need to make clear the level of scrutiny to which your paper was subjected, even non-refereed pieces can help to build careers and reputations, especially in the early stages.

What makes a publishable paper?

Even though the types of refereed papers that you might publish can vary enormously, there are generic qualities that journal editors and referees look for in all of them. Good publishable papers will have a majority, if not all, of the following characteristics. This list is adapted from Kenway *et al.*, *Publishing in Refereed Academic Journals* (1998):

- They present new knowledge, either in the form of substantive research findings, theoretical developments, new insights into existing debates, new analyses of existing knowledge or a synthesis of the literature.
- They are grounded in the relevant literature, demonstrating familiarity and engagement in an on-going academic conversation.
- They address new or familiar issues pertinent to the discipline or field.
- They ask and attempt to answer provocative questions in a persuasive manner.
- They are well written, with carefully crafted and sustained arguments.

How do I get my paper published?

Taking a paper from the first twinkle in your eye through to publication is, unfortunately, quite a long and complicated process. Below we take you through the seven stages from start to finish. Figure 1 presents these stages in diagrammatic form.

Stage one: getting ideas, doing research and writing

If you haven't even started on this stage, you need to read *Getting Started on Research* and also Chapter 2 of this book.

Stage two: giving conference and seminar papers

Once you have developed a paper you really need to take it on the road – taking it to conferences, seminars and workshops. Within reason, a good paper can't have too many outings – but watch that you don't give the same paper to the same people again and again. We deal with conference papers in detail in *Building Networks*.

It's important to use conferences, seminars and workshops as a way of getting feedback so that you can reflect on, refine and polish your paper until you have buffed it up enough to be sent to a journal. You can

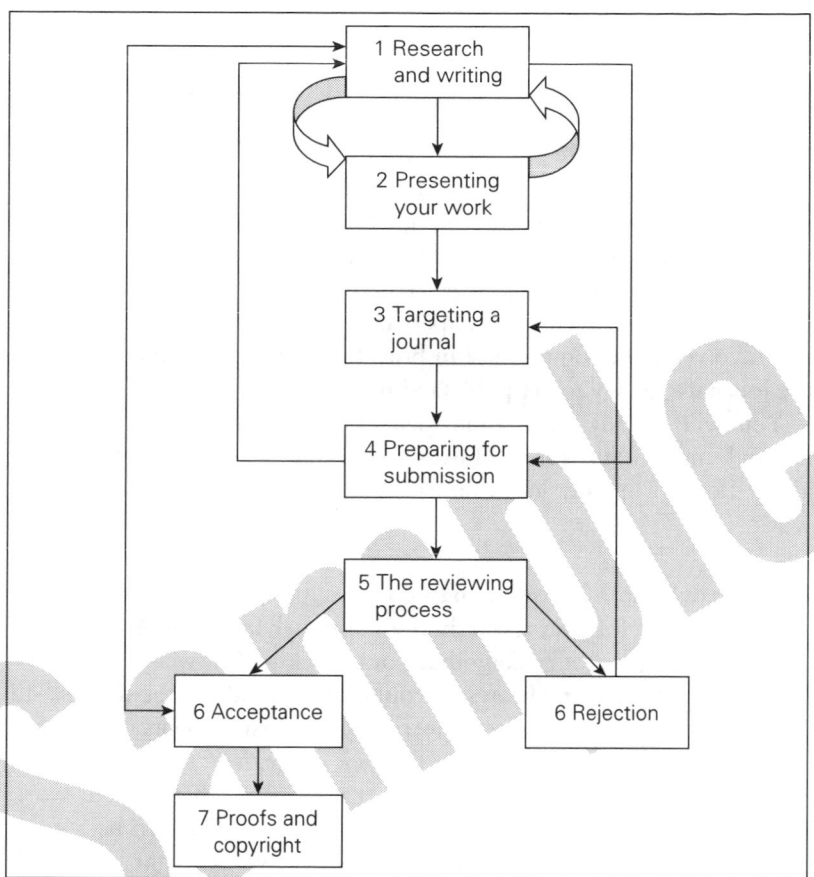

FIGURE 1   Seven steps to heaven: Stages in getting a paper published

be sure that if you keep getting similar adverse comments when you present the paper, your reviewers will also discern the weaknesses when you submit it unless you have resolved the problems. It may be a matter of explaining more carefully what you mean or addressing more fundamental issues. On the other hand, if your paper stimulates lively discussion and interest, it signals that you have struck a rich seam from which to publish. Be careful to take good notes on what people say about your work. Write these up either during your session or immediately afterwards. If you feel that you can't cope with presenting your paper, answering questions on it and taking notes of people's comments and suggestions, get a friend or colleague in the audience to do the note taking for you.

Stage three: targeting a journal

Okay, you have written a paper that has been well aired, commented upon and subsequently and iteratively improved. Now you need to identify an appropriate journal to eventually send it to.

Finding the right journal takes time and effort. But investment at this stage will save you much energy and grief later on. Not all journals, as you will be aware, are the same. They embody different areas of interest, styles, methodologies, aims and objectives. You must achieve a reasonable degree of congruence between your paper and the target journal. Inevitably this involves some compromise in both how you rewrite the paper and the journals you try to get published in.

You will already have some idea about journals from your own research and reading for it. However, here are some more suggestions about how to initially locate journals that may be interested in your work.

- You could do a lot worse than consider the journals that you have been reading for your research. If you find what they publish interesting and relevant, it is likely that your work will fit well.
- Go to the library and browse through the journals on the shelves. All of them will have notes for contributors and statements of editorial policy, usually inside the front or back cover. You should also scan the articles in their back issues to get a sense of whether your work is congruent with the journal's remit and style. This can be a good way of shaping your thinking about where work might be placed. Be imaginative and a bit eclectic about what you look at and don't necessarily confine yourself to a narrow sphere of interest.
- Go to the websites of the substantial publishers of journals and look through their lists of journals. Various search engines, especially in library databases of journals, will take you to these sites. There you will be able to search for journals in particular disciplinary or interest areas. Each journal will have its own page, including its editorial policy, sample issues and articles (for free download) and notes for contributors.
- Ask your mentors or more experienced colleagues for suggestions. But beware – the increasing preponderance of research quality measurement exercises has often tended to lead to a mindless, lemming-like rush for certain journals that achieve iconic status. If your work fits nicely with such journals, all well and good.

However, we would strongly counsel against twisting and distorting your papers in order to try to squash them into a particular journal box they do not fit.

- Sign up for the various journal electronic alert lists that are available. These can take the form of simply giving you the contents pages of journals in your sphere of interest, or may give you abstracts of articles. You can put in your own key words and, provided you choose them sensibly, this will be a useful way of finding out which journals publish your kind of stuff.

Handy hints for targeting journals

We have told you how to look for journals, but what exactly are you looking for? Remember that you need to take a really focused, strategic approach to this important task.

1. The stated editorial policy and your impression of the papers carried should give you a clear picture of the kinds of themes and issues that the journal seeks to address. Eliminate those journals that really have no interest in your areas of concern, broadly construed.
2. Sometimes journals have a particular epistemological, theoretical or indeed political leaning, either stated or unstated. By and large, you should respect these stances and not send your work to a journal that is patently out of sympathy with your own stances. On the other hand, sometimes you may be pleasantly surprised to find that journals with a reputation for publishing only papers of a certain type would actually welcome a broader range of submissions. This is most likely to be the case where the editorial approach is non-positivist because, by its nature, such thinking is open to differing notions of knowledge creation (see also *Getting Started on Research*). If in doubt, it's always worthwhile contacting the editors and sending them a short abstract of your article to check out whether it is the kind of thing that, in principle, they would consider.
3. Journals have different attitudes to publishing a range of styles of writing. Some will welcome experimental writing or poetry. Others are committed to the standard academic generic forms. If you have

written something experimental or unconventional, there is little point in sending it to a journal that does not and will not include that kind of writing.

4. Look at the list of editors and the editorial board to see whether the people included do your kind of work or are interested in it. Some journals also publish an annual list of people not on the editorial board who have reviewed papers for them. It's worth looking at this to see what kinds of people are receiving the papers. Don't send a paper to a journal that regularly uses reviewers who might be unsympathetic to your work and/or your area.

5. There are a number of practical issues to which you must also pay attention. For instance, journals accept articles of different lengths. Some want very short submissions while others are prepared to accept much longer articles. This will be stated in the guidelines for authors inside the back or front cover of the journal and on their web page. Failure to heed these guidelines makes editors very grumpy.

6. Journals have different turn-round times for the refereeing process and lead times for publication when accepted. Sometimes this information appears in the journal itself as a footnote to each paper. There are a number of complex factors that impact on lead times. The vagaries of research quality assessment exercises can mean that there is a rush to publish before the exercise deadlines, swamping journals. Sometimes editors seek to cluster papers that they think fit well together. Putting an edition of a journal together can be a complex jigsaw puzzle, especially as editors are limited in the number of pages they are allowed to have in each issue. This means that you may be moved up or down the queue, depending on the length of your paper, as they try to make the most economical use of the space available. If getting your work out within a tight period is crucial to you, then you should check out all these issues with the editor before you submit. New journals can be a good place to send your articles if you want them out quickly, as they are often in search of good material in order to make an impact with their early issues.

7. You should keep an eye open for information about upcoming special issues that may suit your work. These will be put together within a particular time frame and the guest editors often need to solicit, review and accept the appropriate number of articles quite quickly.

8. Pay attention to whom the journal is aimed at. It is, for example, a waste of time to send an article that has relevance only within your own national boundaries to a journal that promotes itself as being about genuinely international issues.

9. An increasing number of journals charge authors for submission or publication of papers. These charges can be substantial. If your institution does not pick up such fees, or you have to negotiate it, then that is another consideration in your journal selection. It is also a consideration to be built into any research funding applications.

10. Conversely, in the UK at least, funds exist to encourage journals to publish papers from academics in low to middle-income countries. Moreover, journals gain international prestige by showing that they attract authors from a wide range of countries. What can sometimes look like a closed shop isn't necessarily so.

11. Don't waste your time and energies trying to get published in a journal if you have had a huge argument with the editor. Conversely, try not to fall out with important journal editors.

12. Try to pick journals that you wish your name and work to be associated with – generally those that will help you to gain prestige and academic standing in a particular area. Thus journal selection becomes an important part of your networking and career-building work.

13. As time goes on and you build up your publications record, spread your wings a bit and don't always publish in the same place or places. At the same time, it is good to develop a relationship with the editors of particular journals, and you may want to publish in some places more than others. The key here is to keep the right balance.

14. Get to know editors by getting yourself introduced to them or going to their presentations at conferences. You can help to build up a good relationship with journals by undertaking what are sometimes regarded as thankless tasks, such as doing book reviews. As time goes on, and you get more established, you may be asked to be a reviewer or referee for articles submitted to the journal. It's always a good idea to be helpful and amenable in doing such work because then you will be regarded as a good friend of the journal. It won't mean that bad papers get published or that you will have an easier ride, but it may help to ensure that you and your papers are dealt with promptly and efficiently.

Again, this is part of building a network within your academic community (see *Building Networks* for more on this). Having such a relationship will help you to approach the editor with your ideas and have constructive discussions about how to take them forward.

15. The single most important thing in choosing where to publish is to select journals which suit your work, which you are interested in and which allow you to make the best possible impact. Other things being equal, however, try to target the most prestigious journal that you realistically have a chance of getting your work into.

Journals are often ascribed 'national' or 'international' labels. As a matter of course, virtually all journals seek to be seen as international. If we started picking at the thread of what makes a journal national or international, we could fill the rest of this book. Ultimately, whether a journal is of national or international importance is a matter of judgement. The international relevance of research, even if it deals with a local subject, is a key marker of excellence. For journals, an international dimension is a necessary but not sufficient condition for excellence. That international dimension might be connoted by the breadth of the editorial board and the origins of the articles but, most important, by whether the papers themselves are capable of speaking to audiences beyond narrow national boundaries.

Stage four: preparing your paper for submission

The task of preparing your paper for submission to a journal is quite complex; Figure 2 shows the process. Preparing a paper for submission involves the synthesis of three important constituent elements: your pre-existing paper, the feedback that you will have received on it and the specific requirements and characteristics of your target journal. We call this process 'drafting and crafting'. What you will be doing is gently moulding your paper so that it is beautifully written, academically robust and irresistible to your target journal. When you have done this, you will need one last round of polishing before your 'baby' is ready to go off.

For this stage you should already have the draft paper, feedback and journal requirements to hand. You can't start without them. There are two key aspects to drafting and crafting: content and form. Both need

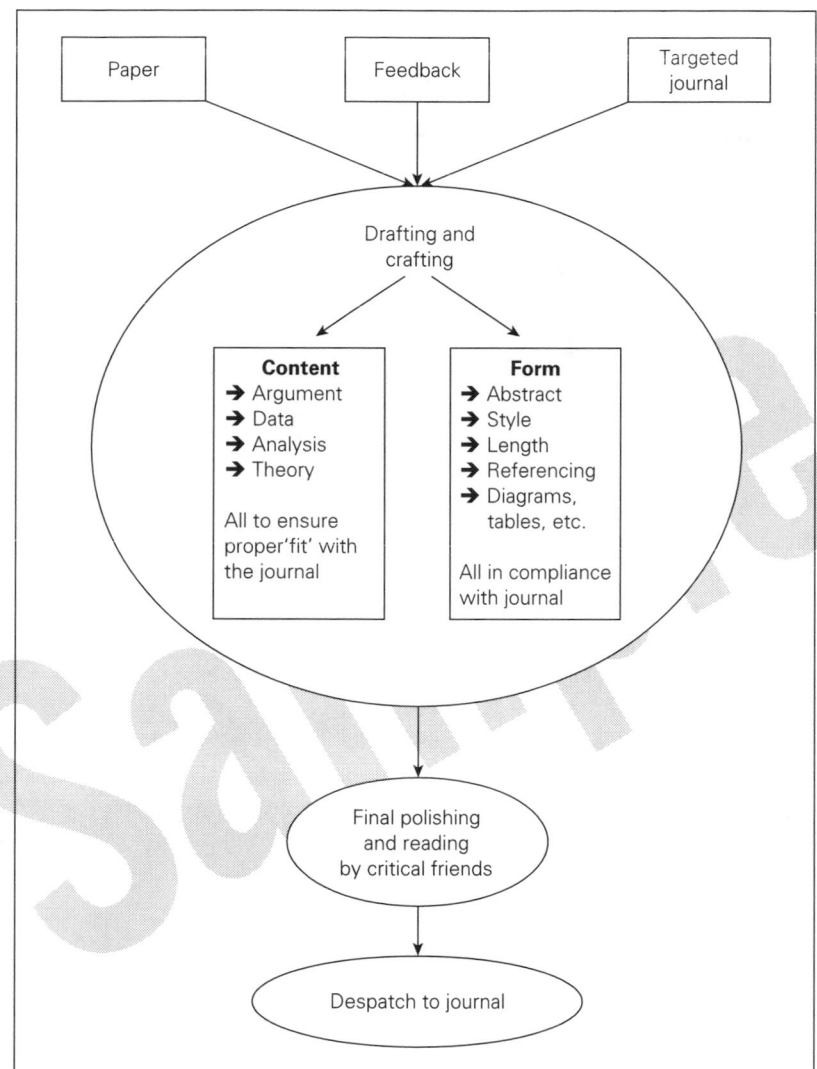

FIGURE 2   Preparing a paper for submission to a journal

to be carefully addressed if you are to be successful in getting your work published. The two textboxes below give you a checklist of things that you have to pay close attention to. You may also find it helpful to refer to *Getting Started on Research* and Chapter 2 of this book.

Content

- Has your paper got a carefully sequenced, logically organised argument that fits together and works like the finest Swiss clockwork? If so, is it explicit, so that you minimise the amount of work the reader has to do?
- Is there a clear and strong relationship between the argument and any evidence, data or other material that you have used?
- Is your analysis of any evidence, data or other material methodologically sound, clearly described and well justified?
- Have you drawn on appropriate theoretical resources and used them in ways that elucidate your arguments rather than obscure them? Are you sure that you have properly understood the theory that you have used? Do not, on any account, rely on derivative writings, as interpretations by others may be misleading or inappropriate.
- Overall, does your paper 'sit' well with the kind of work published in the journal and your intended audience?
- Finally, and most important, is your work credible as a publishable paper, albeit possibly with some revision? You must on no account use the journal review process instead of doing the drafting and crafting work yourself with the assistance of critical friends/mentors/advisers/supervisors and taking the paper around to conferences and seminars.

Form

- The overwhelming majority of journals require an abstract along with the paper. This is a very short (usually 150–200 words) summary of what the paper says. Abstracts are important because, if or when your paper is published, the abstract will be used by potential readers in deciding whether your work may be of value to them. Reviewers of your paper may also utilise the abstract as part of their work. Brevity does not mean that this is an easy thing to get right. Make sure that the abstract matches what the paper is actually about.

- Have you written your paper in the designated house style of the journal? For example, have you complied with guidelines on matters such as capitalisation, the spelling conventions, the use and positioning of footnotes and/or endnotes, punctuation and so on?
- It is vital that you adhere rigorously to the designated referencing style of the journal, so that all your references are complete, none has been omitted and there are no redundant ones from earlier drafts. This will be easy if you have taken our advice in *Getting Started on Research* and invested in a good bibliographic database package. Otherwise, you will just have to be pedantically methodical and careful. Failure to adhere to referencing guidelines is a major source of aggravation for editors and a good way to get on their bad sides. Consider it to be one of the Seven Deadly Sins.
- Is the layout of your paper on the page clear and comprehensible? Does it follow the guidelines for the journal? For instance, most journals ask you to include diagrams, graphs, pictures and so on as appendices with a note in the text where the typesetters should insert them. Usually journals request that the manuscript is double-spaced and that your name does not appear anywhere other than on the title page (except possibly in the bibliography, although you may choose to insert 'author' here instead of your name). We explain below why this is an important requirement.
- Is your paper a suitable length for the journal? Sometimes this is expressed as the number of words (usually by non-US journals), whilst US journals commonly use a page (i.e. 'letter size') length. Watch out for the fact that US paper sizes can vary quite markedly from those used elsewhere.
- Are your diagrams, graphs, figures, tables, pictures and so on clearly labelled, of good quality and obviously related to the written text? Don't rely on colour unless you know that the journal will use colour printing.
- Don't ferget to use the spillchicker. Don't rely on it entirely, as some misspellings don't get picked up. Rebecca once missed a critical 'l' off her curriculum vitae when talking about her 'public sector research'. Grammar checkers is sometimes helpful too, but didn't rely on it because their often wrong.

Your paper is almost ready to go. Whilst we caution against obsessive polishing which actually rubs the gilt off, it is worth while at this stage to get your critical friends and mentors to give the thing a final read over if they have the time and interest. Whilst you should be your own best critic by this stage, they may pick up on things that you, because of your closeness to the work, have missed. If time permits, put your paper away for a few days and then come back to it with fresh eyes and re-read it. A little bit of distance can really help you to see the wood for the trees. At this point you may do a bit of final tweaking, but it shouldn't be much. This may all sound like hard work, and it is. But you should be proud of your work and want it to be seen in the best possible light.

Finally, at last, you are ready to despatch it. All journals make it a condition of submission that the article is being sent only to them. Abide by this rule or you will lose credibility with editors and peer reviewers. There is a sensible reason for it – the reviewing process is time-consuming and expensive hard work for all involved. Nobody wants to go though it, thinking they are helping you, when you are in fact two-timing them.

You now have to write a letter to the editor. We think that it is a good idea to introduce yourself if you are likely to be unknown to them. If you do know them (perhaps because you have been doing good networking work at conferences, etc.) then remind them where they met you and perhaps what they said. If they know your doctoral supervisor/adviser or mentor, then remind them of that too. Don't be pushy, but do exude a nice quiet confidence that you are a worthy author moving in the right circles and doing interesting things. Tell them a little bit about what the paper is about (maybe just one sentence), but don't repeat the abstract. It can also be helpful to explain a bit of the paper's background – perhaps that it is derived from work on a major funded project or how you came to be doing it. Keep all this networking and contextual information very brief.

Check the journal's requirements regarding submission – do they want hard copies (if so, how many) and a computer disk or are they willing to accept electronic copies only? If so, will they accept them by email or do they want a disk? Keep your own copies of what has been despatched. Make a note of the date, but do bear in mind that the next stage (see below) can take a very long time, so you need to put it towards the back of your mind and not worry. Finally, put it all in the post/send the email and go out and celebrate in whatever way floats your boat.

Stage five: the waiting game – the review process

We thought you might find it useful to have a description of what happens to your paper while you are doing all that waiting.

When the journal editor receives your paper the first thing that they will do is to give it a quick read-over to check the following things:

- That the paper is in the right area for the journal and that, for example, you are not a dentist who has accidentally sent a paper to the *International Journal of Oral History*.
- It is in the required format for the journal or near enough so that it is worth sending out for review.
- Whether it is intended for a special issue or the regular journal, and any other exceptional issues that you may have raised in your covering letter.
- Most important, they will check whether it is of a sufficiently high standard to be worth sending out to review. Editors are very aware of how hard academics work and of what a lot of work it is to review a paper properly. They don't want to alienate their all-important pool of reviewers by sending out papers that wouldn't pass an undergraduate examination.

Gender and Education is the leading feminist journal in education. As such, it is committed to assisting inexperienced and/or unsupported academics to be able to publish in it. The journal rule is that all articles must be reviewed by at least one member of the 20-member editorial board. It became apparent that the review process of the journal was being used by authors as a kind of work avoidance, with too many half-baked papers being sent in and reviewed time and time again. This placed an intolerable burden on the editorial board and, indeed, on other reviewers. As a result, the board decided that papers could no longer be resubmitted more than once.

A good editor who is unhappy with your paper at this stage will send it back to you with a letter of explanation. Once the editor is satisfied, they will do two things. First, they will send you an acknowledgement informing you that they have received your paper and sent it out for review. If you have sent a paper off and don't hear anything for a month, it is worthwhile emailing the editor politely to double-check that the paper has actually been received. However, you should not hassle and harry. Second, they (or their administrative assistant) will remove the title page with your name on it from the manuscript. They will also check to make sure that your name doesn't appear in other places, such as the headers or footers, and that you have not cited yourself in ways that identify you as the author. If you are identifiable in any way, they may well ask you to resubmit the paper rather than compromise the blind peer review process.

The editor will then give it a reference number and send it to at least two selected referees together with the journal's evaluation sheet, which asks them to comment on various aspects of your paper and to indicate whether it is publishable. Part of their response will be intended for your eyes but the editor may also offer them the opportunity to make comments just for the editor's eyes.

Who are these referees? They will usually be experienced academics and researchers whose expertise fits them well to critically evaluate the suitability of your paper for publication. Although they will not officially know who the author of a paper is, they may well be able to guess if they have been busy out and about at conferences or reading the journals in which you have previously published. They will usually not be people in your own institution or whose help you acknowledge, although this has been known to occur.

The reviewers will be asked to return the paper within a limited period – often about six weeks. However, because this is the kind of work that academics struggle to find space to do, papers for review often get relegated to the bottom of the pile and they do not manage to meet their deadlines. What this means is that the poor old editor (or their administrative assistant) will have to write reminding them that they have a paper to review. How quickly such a reminder is sent out after the due date for the review depends very much on the journal's administrative resources. You can help yourself here by submitting the best possible paper that precisely meets the journal's requirements. A well written paper on an interesting topic will incite the reviewer to do their work much more promptly than one that they approach with dread terror. This is another reason to write a really sparkly abstract, as nine of out ten reviewers will at least scan it when they open the envelope/attachment from the editor before putting the article at the bottom of their overflowing in-tray.

It has to be said that reviewers vary in quality. Some do a wonderful job whilst others are vindictive, destructive and self-obsessed or just plain lazy. They are so heterogeneous that we can't begin to describe the gamut of behaviours. However, we give you below two completely fictional pen portraits of the Reviewer from Hell and the Reviewer as Angel.

The Reviewer from Hell

Professor Nick Beelzebub is not really an active researcher and is living on his past reputation. However, he always agrees to undertake reviews because he enjoys the power it gives him as a gatekeeper over his younger and evidently brighter peers. He delights in tearing a paper to pieces without making any constructive suggestions for revision. He is firmly fixed in his own research paradigm and will not countenance any alternatives. His comments on others' papers always start from the premise that they should have adopted his favoured approach and the fact that they haven't means that the research is valueless. That is, he never judges anybody's work on its own merits but only by reference to his own beliefs. The reviews are peppered with unfortunate and hurtful phraseology such as 'the author completely fails ...', 'this is weak and insubstantial work' and so on. Old Nick has no regard for the feelings of the nervous authors who will be receiving his commentaries. It is either impossible to divine from his reviews what needs to be done to make the paper publishable or his demands are completely unrealistic and inappropriate.

The Reviewer as Angel

Professor Angelica Hope is a successful academic, who is quietly confident about her own abilities and expertise. She undertakes reviewing work assiduously although she has trouble fitting it in with her heavy work load. This means that she sometimes keeps papers for longer than she would really wish to. Her comments are invariably honest, straightforward and constructive. She aims to help authors

▶ present their own work and ideas in the best way for them and the journal. When asking for a paper to be revised, she will give very clear and precise advice on how to go about it. She may recommend additional literature that would be useful or further analysis work. When she has finished writing her comments, she carefully rereads them and tries to imagine herself as the author receiving them, asking herself the question 'How would I feel if these comments were about my work?' This doesn't mean that she never has negative things to say. Furthermore, if she really thinks that a paper is unsalvageable, she will say so and explain why.

Once the editor has, eventually, received the reviewers' comments they can make a judgement about what should happen to your paper. The editor's job is a crucial one at this stage, as they may have to arbitrate between reviewers who disagree or make judgement calls about how much they should encourage you to revise the paper and resubmit it to them. Whatever the decision, the editor will write to you explaining it and enclosing any reviewers' comments. Opening that envelope/email can stimulate emotions from ecstasy to despair and dread terror and/or extreme anger. These emotional reactions are never completely attenuated, no matter how senior people become. You need to allow yourself to have the reaction but then think about how to move your paper along. A number of different sorts of editor's decisions are possible.

Scenario 1, and very unlikely, your paper may be accepted as it stands with no revisions or amendments. Let's be frank, this is very unusual so don't beat yourself up if it doesn't happen to you.

Scenario 2, the editor may accept the paper subject to relatively minor amendments that do not require it to be sent out for review again. The sorts of things you might be asked to do are, for example, to clarify the use of diagrams or graphs, to define your terms better, to strengthen the introduction or conclusion, to rewrite the abstract more clearly or to improve the referencing. This is far from an exhaustive list – it's just meant to give you a feel for the kinds of things regarded as minor revisions.

Scenario 3, and a very common category, you may be asked to make major revisions and then resubmit for reconsideration by reviewers.

Here the kinds of revision required will be more substantive and may require quite significant reworking either of the theory or data analysis or the structure of the paper. Reviewers should give you quite detailed and clear feedback on exactly what needs to be done and you need to pay careful attention to it.

Scenario 4, your paper may be rejected outright. Rather like asking someone you really fancy out on a date, rejection invariably hurts. There are many types of rejection and many reasons why a paper may be rejected. For instance, the paper may be deemed inappropriate for the journal. If that happens, you should not have had to wait too long, as a good editor should have picked this up before sending it out for review. In such a circumstance, some editors will offer suggestions of alternative journals to which you might submit the paper. Alternatively, the paper may be deemed irredeemably poor and not capable of sufficient improvement to make it publishable in that particular journal. Remember that no judgement is truly objective and that the reviewers' and editors' decisions may be prompted by fundamental epistemological or theoretical differences – they may simply not see the world in the same way that you do. Alternatively, the quality of your work may not have been very good and the reviewers should explain clearly in what ways your paper is deficient.

> Barry received a hurtful rejection on a piece of important work that he had been doing. He realised that he had sent it to the wrong journal when one reviewer wrote, 'Why does the author keep saying things like "Our interviews showed" – qualitative interviews can show "nothing"!' Barry subsequently revised the paper slightly and it appeared in a prestigious edited collection.

Stage six: what happens next? Acceptance or rejection

So you have heard back from the journal on the outcome of the reviewing process and have received the editor's decision. When there is no consensus among the reviewers as to what should happen to the paper, the editor should provide a lead. This is usually phrased something like 'I suggest that you concentrate on Reviewer A's comments.' If there is disagreement between reviewers and the editor does not give a lead, then you should contact her or him to clarify exactly what they want you to do.

> Anwar received the editor's letter and reviewers' comments on a paper he had submitted to a journal special issue. The decision was that he should revise and resubmit the paper for further reviewing. When he read the reviewers' comments, he realised that the two sets of suggestions would take the paper in completely opposite directions and that he could not possibly fulfil both reviewers' requirements. However, the guest editors of the journal had not indicated to him which reviewer to focus on. When he asked what to do, he was told that he should make his own decision on this, so he followed the suggestions that were more in line with his own thinking. The resubmitted paper was sent back to the reviewers. One reviewer (and you can guess which) pronounced the paper much improved and recommended publication without further ado and as a matter of urgency because of its immediate importance. The other reviewer said that unfortunately the changes made to the paper had 'rendered it unpublishable'. Happily for Anwar, the editors decided to follow the first reviewer's opinion.

What you do once you receive a response from the journal depends upon which of the scenarios listed above your paper falls into. Let's go through each in turn.

Scenario 1, unconditional acceptance. In this case there is nothing to do at this stage except celebrate.

Scenario 2, accepted subject to minor revisions. You need to pay very close attention to what you have been asked to do and think carefully about how to respond to each suggestion. You shouldn't make compromises that make you feel uncomfortable or that you don't agree with, but you shouldn't be truculent or resistant to what may well be sensible suggestions. When you have finished the revisions, write an itemised letter to the editor setting out how you have addressed each and every request for revision. If you have declined to follow any particular revision, you need to explain in detail why.

Scenario 3, revise and resubmit. Here the suggestions are likely to be more general than specific and will undoubtedly require quite a lot of work. Again, you need to think carefully about what has been suggested and you may well need to take advice from your mentors and critical friends on how to approach the task. Again, when you have finished your rewrite, you need to construct a careful letter to the editor explaining how you have addressed the reviewers' comments. This letter will normally be sent back out to the reviewers with your revised paper. Your paper will then go through the same process as before, often being returned to the original reviewers. If you have done the job properly your next letter from the editor should be of scenario 1 or 2 type.

Scenario 4, outright rejection. You need to take a cool, long look at the reasons why your paper was rejected. It may take a little while before you feel able to do so, as you will undoubtedly feel hurt, undermined, angry or offended (or some combination of these) by the rejection. It is particularly important that you do return to your paper to see how it could best be salvaged. If you have taken our advice so far, it is likely that with sufficient effort you will be able to make a publishable paper out of it.

Having reappraised your paper in the light of the feedback you have received on it, and after taking advice from suitably experienced colleagues, you may genuinely believe that the rejection was a product of unfair reviewing, ideological conflicts or even personal animosity. In such circumstances you should send the paper, perhaps with some revision in the light of feedback, to another journal.

If, however, you realise that the paper was indeed very weak, you need to decide whether or not you can actually rescue it. This will involve you going back to the drawing board to restart the process at an appropriate point. How far back you go will depend on how bad you think your paper is and the reasons for the problems with it.

> Stacey had recently completed her PhD and developed her first substantive journal paper from it. She received a crushing and ineptly worded set of brusque comments back from the reviewers and an outright rejection from the editor. In consequence, it took her a while ▶

▶ to regain her self-confidence and equilibrium. She took the paper to one of her senior colleagues, who she felt would be able to advise her. He suggested resubmitting the paper to a journal in a completely different disciplinary area where Stacey had no particular expertise, although she had called upon some of the theoretical resources of that discipline. She was uncomfortable with the advice, as it seemed to her that it did not take her or her paper seriously, was quite dismissive and had little chance of being a successful strategy. She went to another senior colleague, who spent some time helping Stacey to address the serious weaknesses in her line of argument so that she could resubmit the paper to a journal in her own disciplinary field. At the same time, she procured technical assistance from another experienced colleague who helped her address the criticisms of the statistical data in her paper. Clearly, reworking the paper at this level is taking her some time, but she has much more chance of success this way.

Stage seven: the technicalities of proofs and copyright

Once your paper has finally been accepted there will be what will probably feel like an age (and may actually be one) before anything seems to happen. Editors like to have a substantial number of accepted papers 'in the bag' in order to give themselves flexibility in putting each edition of the journal together and to save themselves nightmares about not having enough papers to publish. When things finally happen, you will be expected to act yesterday. It usually goes something like this. All of a sudden, when you are least expecting it, are about to give birth or go on holiday, you will receive printer's proofs. These are copy pages of the paper as it will appear on the page in the published journal. These days they are likely to be sent electronically as a read-only PDF file.

The editor will ask you to check the proofs for spelling errors, serious omissions of chunks of text, missing or inaccurate references, etc. If you have done your job properly up to now, you should have very little work to do at this stage unless something has gone wrong with the typesetting – unlikely but it does happen. However, you do need to proof-read very carefully and don't get so carried away with the beauty of your own prose that you miss glaring typos. Editors will be furious with you if, at this stage, you seek to make amendments (rather than typographical corrections) to the text. And rightly so – the technicalities of actually putting a journal together are immense and amendments at this stage can be financially costly. If you really do need to make an amendment it will need careful and sensitive negotiations with the editor to see if it is feasible.

Along with the proofs, you will receive a copyright assignment form. We dealt with the issue of intellectual property rights (IPR) in Chapter 3. You and any co-authors will be asked to sign the form and return it with the proofs. This form is very important, as without it the publishers will not go to press with your article in case you sue them for breach of copyright.

Both the proofs and the copyright matters need to be dealt with as a matter of urgency – usually within two or three days of receipt.

4   Teaching Identities

In this chapter we attend to some issues that are central to your work as a teacher – developing your teacher identity, building your teaching portfolio and managing your time.

Developing yourself as a teacher

You should aim to plan the development of your experience and profile as a teacher in exactly the same proactive way as you should your research (see *Getting Started on Research*). The list we will shortly give you of what might be included in your teaching portfolio offers some insight, we think, into the sorts of activities you should be undertaking and the experience you should be seeking to acquire. As you compile your portfolio you will be able to identify where the gaps and overlaps are. Try to make sure that you have a balanced portfolio with no major omissions.

Work load

Try to take some reasonable control over the direction that your teaching career is travelling in. With regard to the overall shape of your teaching work load, you should plan your teaching commitments with care and in consultation with your colleagues, mentors and managers. You shouldn't be asked, or offer, to take on too many new courses in a year. When you take a course over, it should be on the understanding that you will keep it for a reasonable period: the start-up costs involved with beginning or taking over a new course can be very high and you need to get some economies of scale. Don't spread yourself too thinly. Teaching on too many courses means that you can't give your proper attention to any of them or to the students on them.

People are often scared of undertaking teaching in new areas. We would not recommend that you develop new courses or take on new teaching in areas in which you have no interest. However, developing new courses can be interesting and exciting for you if you are interested in the field, even if you don't yet have specialist expertise. It is a great way to get into new areas of literature. Having to teach a subject really forces you to make sure that you understand it. In some departments there may be real obstacles to developing new courses. For instance, colleagues anxious to defend their own territory or to defend student numbers enrolled on their own courses. The more universities cut back on staffing, the more vulnerable staff will feel. You have to negotiate your way through this, patiently, carefully and diplomatically, remembering that you don't have a God-given right to teach any course you like regardless of your colleagues' interests or the course's viability. Courses with very small student numbers are costly to run and the university is unlikely to support you in developing them.

Technical skills

Try to make sure that your technical skills are suitably and frequently updated and are what you require. This applies especially to IT, which is a fast moving environment. IT can provide a powerful range of tools that can really make teaching more effective, flexible, interesting and accessible. Conversely, don't be seduced into spending huge amounts of time learning fancy new IT skills that really, when you are honest with yourself, don't actually contribute much to your teaching. We all have colleagues who spend endless hours doing more and more sophisticated PowerPoint presentations with animation and sound effects who actually deliver pretty prosaic and boring lectures that are a triumph of form over content.

The more universities understand their capacity to attract a broader student base as a function of technology, and the more student numbers increase, the more the pressure is on teaching staff to put all their courses on-line and to do more and more on-line teaching. One of the arguments made here is that it is a flexible approach that attends to the needs of students. This may or may not be the case. There are several things to keep in mind under such circumstances, one of which relates to the IT issues mentioned above. However, there are broader peda-gogical questions that you, as a teacher, need to resolve:

- What is best taught on-line and what is not?
- What are the best ways of teaching on-line?
- What technology and what technological competencies do you and your students have and need?

Don't make the mistake of assuming that the pedagogies that you adopt in face-to-face teaching automatically transfer successfully to the on-line environment. Neither should you make the big mistake of thinking that teaching on-line will save you time or effort. It is, in fact, one of the most demanding forms of teaching you can do in both these respects. All that said, it is useful to keep in conversation with those who are at the leading edge in the use of IT in teaching because they will know about the latest software packages that might well enhance your teaching on-line.

In thinking about the relationship between teaching and technology, don't forget that there are a variety of technologies at your disposal. They include such 'old-fashioned' things as the telephone, video, film or audio recordings and the well worn and trusty overhead projector (which is less likely to let you down than your slick PowerPoint presentation).

Training to teach

Increasingly, new academics are required to undertake some formal teacher training. If the course is good, which sometimes they are, you may find it genuinely supportive and helpful. If it is bad, which they sometimes are, you just have to get through it as best you can. If you have a choice as to whether and which course to attend, then do your homework on their quality and choose the one that suits your needs and style.

In the UK, there is government pressure to formalise the training and continuing professional development of university teachers. A national body, the Institute of Learning and Teaching, has been established to accredit university teachers. In order to get the institution going, the initial route to membership for experienced teachers is less rigorous than is usual for any professional accreditation body. This initial route to membership, originally intended to stand for just one year, has now been extended to three years as academics have experienced some inertia when it comes to applying. There has been considerable pressure from university managers to try and make people join. Sometimes they insist that promotion is dependent upon membership of the ILT. Many universities pay individuals' first-year ▶

membership fee. Many of our less experienced colleagues who have been pressured or coerced into joining the ILT have decided, once they have achieved membership, not to renew it. In this way, they have met their university's requirements, while not colluding with a process for managing teachers with which they fundamentally disagree.

Problematic teaching personalities

Be reflexive about your teaching personality and *modus operandi*. There are two extremes in teaching personality types, both of which you need to avoid. At one end of the scale is the teacher who gives no time outside class and has made an art of positively avoiding and shunning students. Their teaching style in the classroom is likely to be one which holds the students at a distance – constantly talking at the students and taking up all the space and time in the class so as to exclude them. This person is being unfair to their colleagues as well as their students because the follow-on effects of their behaviour will impact on their colleagues. This kind of approach puts pressure on more conscientious teachers to pick up the pieces, tutoring neglected students and dealing with their problems and issues. If you are teaching in such circumstances and this burden becomes too great, then you need to talk to your head of department or mentor about it.

At the other extreme is the teacher who not only mothers but also smothers their students. Jane calls this the problem of the 'eternal breast' – succour (sucker) on demand. You are not your students' mother, their therapist or life coach. Not only are these inappropriate roles for you as a teacher (you may do more harm than good if you are giving advice that you are not qualified to offer) but you are also implicitly creating additional burdens for colleagues by creating unduly high expectations about what staff will do. If you hand out your home phone number to undergraduates, are constantly at their beck and call, read endless drafts of their assignments and generally exceed the boundaries of your real responsibilities, then you create the impression that all your colleagues will do the same. This is an unfair imposition on them. You and your colleagues should mutually agree on the service levels that you give to students and then stick to them except in very unusual circumstances.

If you are a mothering/smothering teacher you really need to look deep inside yourself and decide whether you are doing it because you think it is good teaching practice or because, for your own reasons, you have some real need to be loved and wanted. Playing out such desires has no place in good teaching. That's not to say, however, that you can't and shouldn't get a real kick out of students admiring and respecting you, or even loving you, but you need to keep a balance between necessary availability and care and keeping appropriate boundaries.

One almost parental point from us. Do not, on any account, ever and for any reason become sexually, emotionally or romantically involved with any of your students. We have said enough about the power relations present in the pedagogic relationship to make it self-evident why this is fundamentally abusive. It is generally a good idea to stay well away, in this sense, from *all* students in your university. Personal relationships of this sort are inevitably complicated and, if you must jump into these troubled waters, you need to think very carefully and very deeply before doing so. Furthermore, you must declare your interest with regard to such students in any situation where you may have some influence or be privy to any confidential material about their studies. For instance, you might be on a committee considering their grades or degree classification, and this is clearly problematic.

Building your teaching portfolio

What do you mean by a teaching portfolio?

It is a personal professional record of your teaching that can be used in various ways – as a resource for your teaching and as a record for such things as promotion. Your first year of teaching in higher education in a substantive post, regardless of your previous teaching experience or expertise in the field, is likely to be the single most exhausting and enervating year in your entire career. Everyone goes through it and the good news is that it does get better. There are two reasons why the first year is so hard. One is that you haven't learned the smart tricks that let you get by more easily. More important is that you have little or nothing in your personal teaching bank to call on. You will probably be dealing with new courses and possibly unfamiliar material.

As a resource

Your teaching portfolio provides you with ready access to past work and acts as a sort of teaching savings account on which you can draw (though, unlike your bank account, it won't become depleted when you call on it). So you will want to deposit all the materials that you think will be of future use to you in your teaching portfolio. These teaching banks are also resources that you can share with colleagues and they can share theirs with you. This stops everyone constantly reinventing the wheel, although, of course, you can't abrogate your responsibility to engage directly with and think about your own teaching. You can't pick up and run with someone else's ready-made courses and expect them to work well, notwithstanding the exponential growth in the franchising of teaching materials and courses. You may be in a position in which you are not developing the course on which you teach – for example because you are a graduate teaching assistant, a casually employed teacher or a tutor on a distance learning course such as those run by the UK's Open University. Clearly you have significantly less autonomy in these circumstances and you are unlikely to be free to decide what you teach. You will, however, be able to plan your teaching methods and approaches. The course materials and these plans can all go into your portfolio.

In building your portfolio, you need to keep in mind that universities are now marketised institutions that commodify knowledge. This means that the intellectual products of university staff, such as teaching materials, are increasingly being placed formally and legally under the control of institutions. That is, universities may seek to assert intellectual property rights over your teaching materials. Where this assertion of rights occurs, it seeks to supplant existing collegial systems where professionals shared their materials. For some universities, control over intellectual property is important because they make serious money out of selling courses and franchising them. Your legal situation will vary according to your contract of employment and the law of the country where you are working. You should properly inform yourself about your own situation with regard to IPR on teaching materials. This is particularly problematic for materials that you might place on the intra- or Internet such as lecture notes. Bear in mind that anything to which you give a public material or electronic form may become the university's property. There are two competing traditions at work here. One is that of colleagues sharing teaching materials and acknowledging their provenance. The other is the claim that employers own these materials and can prevent academic staff from freely exchanging materials. Again, we see an example of the ways in which the marketised university can undermine academic freedom and modes of collegiality which enhance teaching.

In *Getting Started on Research* you will find extensive guidance on writing research proposals. This began life when Debbie wrote some shorter guidelines for her master's students at the Institute of Education. Debbie agreed to allow it to be reproduced for a wider student audience. She then shared it with Rebecca, who developed it further and used it in her own masters teaching and then placed it on her university's website to help applicants for doctoral places. Debbie, Rebecca and Jane then used this material in *Getting Started on Research*. The intellectual property rights in that book are shared by us with the publishers. Who has the intellectual property rights in this material?

Interestingly, the material was reproduced at the Institute with no attribution to Debbie. At the University of the West of England, Rebecca claimed the copyright on our behalf. Her university queried it and she insisted that the material could not go on the Web without attribution of copyright to us.

As a record

A further use for your teaching portfolio is that it provides a comprehensive record of your professional teaching practice that you can use for things such as: staff appraisal/performance reviews; promotion applications; tenure applications; and when seeking a new post. You will also find it useful if you need to get your teaching expertise formally accredited.

In assessing your record of teaching achievement, those judging you will be looking at the following sorts of things:

* Good teaching involves the development of original and interesting ideas both for content and for pedagogy. You need to show that you can think not only about what you teach, but also about how you

teach. These ideas will have to be appropriate to the material, your disciplinary area and the students involved.

- One of the things that every competent teacher in higher education should be able to do is to create and mount courses in particular areas, on particular subjects, at various levels.

- As your teaching career progresses, you should be able to demonstrate that you can put together whole degree programmes that have coherence, intellectual integrity and also appeal to students.

- Again, as your teaching career develops, you will be expected to have taught successfully across the complete range of students, from first-year undergraduates to doctoral research students.

- Courses and degree programmes occur within distinct institutional structures and are framed by regulations and university procedures. You must be able to show that you can go further than the drawing board, taking your ideas for teaching, fashioning them and steering them through formal procedures to the point where they become actual programmes.

> Alarmed at the lack of deep intellectual thinking among their masters students, Robert and Andreas designed a reading-based course in which they tried to get the students to engage with the great classical texts in their discipline from the previous fifty years. When they took their proposed course to the relevant university committee for approval, the outline reading list, which they had been required to include, was severely and roundly criticised by managers because it was 'out of date'. Rather than fight people who clearly did not understand the rationale of the course, they simply removed the older of their chosen classic texts from the official documentation and resubmitted it. The course was duly approved. In the documentation that went to the students (and in Andreas and Robert's teaching portfolios) they reinstated all the original texts.

- As a professional teacher in higher education, you should be able to work with others in teams to develop and teach courses. You will need evidence of this in your portfolio.

- Good academics see teaching and research as a seamless web. There is a synergy between teaching and research at both first and higher degree levels. In order to do good research, you will, inevitably, be engaged with and fascinated by your subject. This will enable you to teach it with enthusiasm. You must be able to demonstrate that you have translated your research-led engagement with your subject into your teaching.

- You need to be able to show that the students you have taught feel that they have, for most part, derived enjoyment and benefit from your teaching even if, at times, they found the work difficult, confusing or challenging. In fact, when they find the work challenging, realise there are no right answers and are moved to work hard to try to make sense of things, then you are doing a really good job.

- Finally, the proof of the educational pudding is whether your students generally make satisfactory progress. In managerialist terms, progress means their relative success in passing assessments. However, we think other forms of progress are equally important. These include things like: helping students who might otherwise drop out to stay with the course; assisting all students to achieve their own objectives, even if these don't have much institutional cachet; or making sure that all or most of your students know how to learn for themselves.

What to include in your teaching portfolio

Here is a reasonably comprehensive list. We suggest that these should be on your computer, backed up on disk and also in hard copy. Clearly your teaching portfolio will also include a number of artefacts that can't be kept on your computer.

- *Course outlines*, especially for courses you develop yourself or with others. Keep both the documentation submitted to the university for approval and the stuff that the students actually receive. The official documentation may be useful to you in future if and when you need to go through similar exercises. The documentation for students will demonstrate much better your approach to teaching and your engagement with them.

- *Lesson plans, teaching/lecture notes, overhead projector slides or PowerPoint presentations*. Don't forget to include any agendas or other hand-outs that you have prepared for students.

- Related to your lesson plans will be *activity sheets, games, exercises, teaching aids,* and *seminar notes* for colleagues who teach on your courses, particularly when they are innovative and exciting. Increasingly, university teachers are expected to demonstrate that their programmes are innovative, especially when applying for a new job. As noted earlier, 'innovative teaching' is not synonymous with using digital technologies in teaching, though it may include it. It may also include opening up teaching in new subject areas, developing new teaching methods and/or materials, attracting a new body of students, forging new interdisciplinary links in your teaching.
- *Examples of materials produced by others that you have used.* These will include videos/DVDs, audio material, artefacts, visual images, newspaper cuttings and so on. You will need a note to yourself about how you used them and in what contexts.
- *Student evaluations and other kinds of feedback.* This will vary from formal student evaluation questionnaires that your department or university may insist on (summative assessments) to nice letters from students in which they talk about the impact of your teaching on them. If you are in a position in which you must use the evaluation questionnaires designed by others for management purposes, it is a good idea also to get students to give you additional, formative, feedback in a more useful way for developing your teaching.

Shannon allocates time for students to discuss with her how they feel the course is progressing and makes iterative adjustments in the light of their feedback. In addition to this oral feedback, she asks students at the end of the course to reply in writing to the following three questions:

- What did you enjoy about the course?
- What constructive suggestions can you make for improving it next year?
- Do you have any other comments about the course?

This formative feedback helps her to shape her subsequent teaching.

At the end of each course you should be able to write a short reflection on your own teaching and put it alongside your students' evaluations to contextualise what the students have said. This is particularly important if you feel that the evaluations don't really reflect what went on in the course.

> Often generic university questionnaires are not appropriate for your teaching, your students or your courses. Another disadvantage of such generic feedback forms is that they permit, even encourage, the occasional abusive act by individual students even in the best taught classes and at the best universities. You should not feel obliged to retain, or pass on to anyone else, feedback that is personally abusive or patently troublemaking. You should be aware that it is common for people in certain groups to have had, at least once, anonymous racist, homophobic and/or sexist comments and for all staff to have had adverse comments about their personal appearance, dress sense and so on. The best thing to do with such feedback, if you can't identify the perpetrator, is to treat it with the contempt it deserves. You should also bring such incidents to the attention of the appropriate university authorities. Even if such material does not particularly upset you, other colleagues may be distressed by it, and reporting it may lead to the whole issue being addressed.

- You may have to produce formal *written reports* on your course either for 'quality assurance' purposes or to act as guidance to external examiners or validation bodies. When you are writing such reports, do bear in mind that they have an extremely public audience. Be honest, but be very careful in your phraseology, as bad wording can come back to haunt you. This is not the place for teaching confessions. Everyone screws up from time to time, and you may need to discuss this with a supportive colleague, but you definitely do not need it on the university's official records.
- Your university may have formal mechanisms, such as *course committees or staff–student liaison committees*, where student representatives can give formal feedback on teaching and raise any issues of concern. Minutes of these may be included in your portfolio.

- Examples of the formative *feedback* you give students on their work indicate the quality of your engagement with them. They need to be written to reflect the respect that you show your students in your teaching. Remember that students need a balance of comments that affirm their work and those that suggest ways of improving it.
- Keep a good record of any work of an *administrative nature* related to teaching that you have undertaken. You may have been the director of a degree programme, chair of a student progression committee, responsible for collecting and collating examination marks in your department and so on. Demonstrating that you have done such work and done it well will enable you to show that you are a good colleague and also have a keen understanding of university processes and procedures with regard to teaching.
- University teaching now frequently involves staff in team teaching efforts on specific courses. You might be working with a group of peers or be responsible for co-ordinating the efforts of any number of sessional teachers or Teaching Assistants. Do not underestimate the skills required for this sort of team working and teaching leadership. Keep good records of where you have worked in this way to show that you can and will do it.
- If you have helped and mentored less experienced colleagues in their teaching, it is useful to keep a record of this, in the form of either your own notes or copies of theirs (with their permission).
- If you become known to be a good 'performer' as a teacher, you may well receive invitations to offer specialist classes, or even entire courses, in other departments, faculties or even universities. Keeping records of such work is a marker of the esteem in which your colleagues elsewhere hold you. Similarly, if your course materials are used by other colleagues, either at your institution or elsewhere, keep a note of it.
- If you know that your publications are used in teaching at other institutions, it's useful to have a record of it, for example by getting a copy of the relevant course outlines.
- The more senior you become the more you will be expected to demonstrate not only that you have taught but that you have successful experience of teaching leadership. This may include managing teams of seminar leaders, developing new programmes and courses, introducing new ideas into your courses, leading collaborative teams and managing all the administrative aspects of running large course or degree programmes.

What your mother never told you about time

Everyone we know who works in a university is chronically short of time. Here are some issues to think about in relation to your own time.

Don't forget research. Teaching is, for the most part, a highly structured and formal activity. Apart from one-to-one supervision, tutorials and some aspects of on line teaching you will have to be in a set place, at a set time, with a particular group of students over a particular period. This gives a largely non-discretionary structure to your working week for a significant proportion of the year. This means that you can't ignore teaching and put it on the back burner in the same way that you might do with your research. As such, it's important that you always keep the fact that you have other things to do, such as research, in the foreground of your thoughts and planning. Don't let the formal, compulsory nature of teaching duties swamp out all the other stuff that you must do. This may feel more discretionary because it doesn't occur at fixed times, but it is not.

Busy work and necessary admin. The other activity that has some sort of formal imperative is administration. If you don't submit your exam questions in the appropriate form at the appropriate time, for example, it can cause real problems for all concerned. That said, you need to distinguish carefully between those aspects of the administration of teaching that are truly necessary and important and those which are nothing more than time-wasting trivia. We told you the story earlier on of Boubacar and Achille and their reaction to such 'busy work' (see also *Getting Started on Research*).

Balance your work activities. You may work in a department that has some sort of formal system for the allocation of time between activities such as research and teaching. Some systems just allocate teaching time and expect staff to get on with their research in the time remaining. If you have such a system, try to use it to make sure that you are spending an appropriate proportion of your annual working time on each of teaching, research and administration. You can use these schemes in arguments about work as a justificatory device to make sure that you are not pressured or guilt-tripped into spending undue time on teaching and/or admin.

Timetabling and 'joined up' time. Because you need 'joined up', connected periods of time to get on with your research, it is imperative that your periods of teaching are not spread, like confetti, across the entire week. Timetabling is a real skill and you and your colleagues should work hard with your timetabler to make sure that she or he knows what your needs are. Resist any managerialist system that always prioritises expediency and the needs of 'students as customers'. At an individual level, do your best, when organising your own courses, classes and lectures, to make sure that you protect important research time while still behaving ethically towards students and recognising their legitimate needs. Be a good colleague and, when making teaching arrangements that involve others, bear in mind that your co-workers also need consideration.

Fatu, a lecturer of some years' standing, was struggling to find enough time to complete her doctoral thesis. She taught a second-year undergraduate course and her more senior colleague, Lindsay, taught a related third-year course. Lindsay suggested, for good pedagogical reasons, that they should take some of the seminar groups on each other's courses so that they could develop and maintain better continuity between their two courses for the benefit of the students. The trouble was that all the seminar classes on Lindsay's course were held on the only day of the week that Fatu had otherwise free of teaching and on which she liked to stay at home and work on her thesis. She discussed this with her mentor, who suggested that she explain the problem to Lindsay. Lindsay was very understanding and they agreed to defer their planned swap to the following year, when they could make more mutually satisfactory timetabling arrangements.

It is obviously helpful to be able to get all your teaching on to two or three days in the week if you possibly can. Another good strategy, if you can manage it, is to try to get the bulk of your teaching duties concentrated in one term or semester. We often imagine managing an academic work load as a bit like the old-fashioned circus act, where the performer sets dinner plates spinning on top of poles, the art being to keep as many of them spinning at the same time as possible without letting them crash to the ground. The entertainment value lies in watching the increasingly frantic activity of the performer as they race around maintaining each plate's momentum. This may be entertaining for circus audiences, but it's not much fun as a working life for academics. If you can divide your working year such that you have very concentrated periods of one activity such as teaching, followed by another such as research, you will be far more productive and far less exhausted.

> Miranda was head of a nurse education programme in a university health sciences faculty that was placing increasing stress on research. The programme as it stood involved having both university-based teaching and hospital practice taking place across the whole year. Thus there were always some students needing lectures, seminars and tutorials and others needing to be supervised on their placements. This meant that members of the teaching team had virtually no discretionary time in which they could do their research.
>
> Miranda led her team in a reorganisation of the programme, which meant that the university-based teaching for all students was concentrated into the first semester, while clinical work in hospitals was moved into the second. In the new system, the first semester is very intensive and lecturers have very little time. However, in the second they are able to arrange their own timetables for visiting students in order to give themselves connected, joined-up time to do research. A further advantage is that much of the clinical supervision of students is done by experienced staff in the teaching hospital. This relieves academic staff of their commitments and provides them with much more flexibility.

Research days or research daze. We often find it wryly amusing, when we have been rushing round at our universities all day, teaching, seeing students, going to meetings and dealing with our email, that we get home and say, 'I haven't been able to get any work done today.' Of course, this is ironic. What we really mean is that we haven't had the opportunity to do any sustained intellectual work such as reading, writing or thinking about research or teaching. It's very naughty of us to see all the stuff that we do when we are rushing around in our departments as 'not work'. This is one of the many forms of self-flagellation that academics impose on themselves. Because meetings, seeing students and dealing with routine administrative tasks eat into time, it's best to try to get all that stuff done in the interstices of formal classes. This will leave you free on the days when you are not teaching to stay at home and do some 'real work' uninterrupted. On such days, do not on any account be seduced into 'popping in' to work for anything. It will always take up a good part of the day, if not the whole day. Give your apologies for any meetings on your research days and do not be frightened to prioritise research over meetings. Let it be known what your research days are and make clear to your colleagues that you will not be available for anything on those days under any circumstances. Eventually people get the message. Put your answering machine on and turn your email off.

Teaching, learning and pedagogic praxis. We notice that novice teachers tend to replicate the teaching practices by which they were taught. Practice makes practice, as the Canadian academic, Deborah Britzman, says. And, as Gramsci would say, 'history has congealed into habit' here. It is better pedagogically and in your own best interests to design your teaching (as distinct from scheduling it) in such a way that students quickly become accustomed to taking responsibility for their own learning. For example, if you are teaching students how to do a literature search, consider setting them a group exercise that they have to undertake independently in the library rather than you standing and doing a 'chalk and talk' act. You can always check how well the students have done on the exercise by getting them to do a short presentation back to the class. Many institutions have 'mission statements' and suchlike that espouse the virtues of 'independent learning' and 'student empowerment'. We are inclined to be cynical about such statements, often seeing them as weasel words and managerialist-speak, combined as they usually are with reductionist notions which direct teachers to adopt easily defined 'learning outcomes' and the 'objective measurement' of education. However, when students take real responsibility for their own learning processes, they invariably find it the most educationally satisfying experience that they can have. Equally, as a teacher, it is very rewarding to see students develop in this way.

You should be aware, however, that this kind of teaching does have heavier than usual start-up costs and requires careful preparation.

Students have to be trained and inducted into that sort of approach, especially if they are used to being spoonfed with predigested gobbets of pap-like information. Some students will need additional support to help them adjust to these methods. However, done well, this becomes low-maintenance, low-cost and satisfying teaching.

> Wu was a senior academic in the UK who had strong research links in Australia. During a busy teaching term he needed to go to Australia to pursue his research interests. He spent a few weeks training his seminar students to run their own classes. He equipped them with topics, suitable materials and discussed with them what they would like to achieve. He then went to Australia and let them get on with it on their own. The students in Wu's department regularly voted for a 'Teacher of the Term'. Wu won this accolade during the term in which he ran this experiment and went away. This wasn't an ironic statement by the students (although we tease him that it was); it was just that the students found the whole experience immensely enjoyable and it made them feel as if they were being treated as the mature, responsible people they in fact were.

Some forms of teaching, such as formal lectures, are much more labour-intensive than others. Additionally, many of these types of teaching are actually quite ineffective but tend to be popular with unconfident teachers and lazy students. They therefore have little to recommend them either as a pedagogical device or as a way of getting your work load under control. We say more about lectures below in the section on developing your teaching.

Working at social time. A lot of academic work is quite isolated and lonely. It's a good idea to try, as far as you can, to make busy time at work also act as pleasant social time. You might, for instance, take a lunch or coffee break with colleagues in your own or other departments. A lot of academics we know, including ourselves sometimes, tend to eat a sandwich at our desks. This is really not a good idea – either for your digestion or for your mental well-being. It's better to make a point of going to the coffee bar, canteen or wherever people tend to congregate. That way you get some social interaction and, very often, hear the important gossip, network and actually get some university work done in the process.

Some of the best teaching and research ideas start and are developed over a cup of coffee (or even herbal tea) or lunch. Where small meetings are not confidential, formal or difficult, it's often a good idea to go and have a coffee (or whatever) with the colleagues or students involved. We have had many a productive research meeting or supervision over just such coffee tables – and they can also be the best places to sort out departmental problems (provided you don't need confidentiality). Remember that such social time is not time wasted.

Email is a really important means of communication with colleagues and students all over the world. However, it can also invade your day, fragmenting your time and distracting you from getting on with more substantial tasks. This problem is acute in all walks of professional and commercial life. It is also treacherously easy to think that you must answer an email immediately, without really considering what your answer should be. It is possible to tame this beast. Consider strategies such as opening your email only at a set time each day. On days when you are working at home, consider not looking at your email at all. Pick low value/low energy times to deal with your email correspondence – but if you have an important email to write, don't do it then. Consider having a separate email address for important research projects, significant correspondents or for your personal email.

And finally ...

It's worth pointing out that a teacher identity is something that is built. It comes with time, work and experience. In difficult times, many teachers are tempted to become cynical and jaded in relation to the work. This is understandable but not at all helpful in developing creative strategies for making your teaching a rewarding activity in itself. One of the most satisfying things about being a teacher is the opportunity it provides for you to make a major difference to people's lives. The saying 'everyone remembers a good teacher' has been deployed in advertising campaigns in the UK to recruit schoolteachers, but that does not detract from the fact that it is true. For the jaded and cynical, it is worth remembering that the converse may also be true – few of us forget our really terrible teachers.

In this chapter we have discussed the things you will have to cope with as a teacher and provided you with some advice about how to manage and develop yourself as a teacher. We next consider the teaching associated with postgraduate research students.

6   Project Management

In this chapter we talk you through the project establishment stage and the issues you will deal with as the project proceeds, including working in a team, publishing and dissemination.

Where are you now?

At this point you have heard that you have won the bid. Wild celebrations are in order, of course. Winning is great, and you will be on a high for while, or maybe for the length of the project. But it is not uncommon for people to feel anxious at this stage, particularly if it is their first funded project. You may remember, for instance, all the things you promised – or foolishly over-promised. You may realise what a very hard slog it will be to complete the project and that there will be no relief for the next few years. You may wonder how it will be possible to do the project and all your other work. You may even panic, and with good reason if the research starts Monday next. Well, there is no escaping. You won the money, now you have to do the work. Our task in this chapter is to give you some tips on managing the project well, with the least possible trauma and the best possible results.

The establishment stage

The contract

The contract will accompany any offer of an external funding grant and you must deal with it pronto. It may come with the letter of offer or it may arise after a period of discussion and negotiation with the funder. If the contract is from a funding body such as a research council it will be standard and you can comfortably sign it and your university will do the rest. For other grants you must have your university's legal adviser take a look and help you negotiate any necessary changes. If you are working across several universities each university's legal adviser will have to check it, especially if the money is to go to the separate institutions rather than through one lead university. Prior to doing this, you must check it to see if everything is there and that nothing has changed or been slipped in under your guard. Major matters of concern are time-lines, deliverables and intellectual property.

Also you must attend to things that have changed since you put in the bid. Perhaps the original time-lines have become difficult or the project team may have altered. Under such circumstances the contract needs to be changed and you, or the solicitor, must negotiate this with the funder. Make sure that you can still meet time-lines and that they include everything, particularly the work of the final project stages. Do not get caught doing final revisions to reports after the project is complete and payment over. Funders will vary on the amount of time that is seen as acceptable or necessary between the offering and the signing of the contract and indeed the end of the project and the final report. For instance, the ESRC in the UK insists on a six-week gap between the offer and the signing, and all reports must be submitted three months after the project finishes.

We discuss Intellectual Property Rights (IPR) at length in *Writing for Publication*. In this context you need to think about how to deal with IPR provision in research contracts and make sure it is not only clear from the beginning but does what you want. Don't sign away your right to be known as the researchers and to publish from the project. What you want is the right to:

- Have your team's name and institutions on all the project publications put out by the funder.
- Publish from the project in peer-refereed journals.
- Talk publicly about the project outcomes to your colleagues and the media. You do not want to be gagged for ever – but you may be happy to be gagged for a while to give your funder a chance to read and think about your report.
- Publish the report yourself if the funder refuses to publish it for whatever reason.
- Royalties and other copyright money.

Melissa has done heaps of research and development projects for government education systems. They have involved producing innumerable curriculum and other documents and reports either alone or in teams. She has a fine mind and some astute, practical and original ideas. She also works hard, and in fact usually does most of the work despite being a member of a team. Almost invariably the good ideas are hers. In her early days of doing such government work she was quite naive about matters of IPR. Although she produced a huge amount of curriculum material little had her name on it. Of course this is not unusual in government circles. It did not particularly worry her until she found quite a bit of her work put out under someone else's name. Subsequently she has been much smarter about IPR. Indeed, she recently had a financial windfall from the Australian copyright agency.

Doing budget and project revisions

You don't always get all the money you asked for despite your carefully crafted and totally persuasive budget justifications. Once you know your final amount you must carefully revise your budget for the entire period of the project. This will require you to revise aspects of the project. You cannot try to deliver what you have not been funded for. So downsize your activities and promises and revise your time-line and publishing plan if necessary. Before doing so check to see if your institution can provide you with any top-up money – you may get lucky.

Finding and appointing your research staff

Employ your research and other support staff early. While you can't make or finalise appointments before your contract is through and your budget revised, there are things you can do in advance.

- *Keep your eye open for good people.* Let your colleagues know you need research and/or administrative assistants. They may be able to recommend people to you – but don't just take their word for it. Check out the work of anyone recommended if you can, and do not promise anything until you are in a position to. If you can appoint someone good without going to external advertisement, this is a bonus, as it saves time and money. But it may also mean you do not get the best person. Don't be too hasty to appoint someone just because they are there, warm and upright. You also need to be careful that you don't fall foul of equal opportunities principles and regulations.

- *If you have to advertise,* chat to people in your human resources (personnel) division to see what it entails, how much it costs, and consider what the project can afford now your budget has been revised.
- *Write a preliminary advertisement and job description.* Consider carefully the selection criteria, job description and application time-lines. The personnel people may be able help you do this. Think about who you want to have on the selection committee and line them up informally.
- *Line up all the necessaries* – office and desk space, computers, access keys, telephone access and the like – so that once someone is on board they can get down to work immediately. If you are in a research group or centre, there may be people available to help you do this.

Appointing people is just the start of what you need to do. Once you have them on board you will have to:

- Make sure they have a thorough induction into all those aspects of the university that are pertinent to the project. For example, have them spend some time on the Web getting to know research policies and procedures and in the library, introduce them to the university's email and other systems, and to other researchers, research support staff and research leaders.
- Sit down with them and carefully go though the project, noting particularly time-lines and deadlines. Make sure they understand the project's purposes and the expected outputs.
- Clarify their working hours, role and responsibilities. Make clear what you expect of them and that they are responsible to you.
- Let them know they must plan their holidays and include them within the time of the contract.
- Clarify questions of authorship and ownership with them early. Indicate whether these are negotiable and on what grounds.
- In the context of the time-line, set them to work on a small set of activities, which can be evaluated at the end of that time. Keep a close eye on their work.

- If research assistants are doing research degrees within the project, factor in the fact that they have to be able to identify what work is theirs to legitimately claim their PhD. This is quite difficult and requires very careful and sensitive negotiation and monitoring. Lifelong enmities have arisen out of failure to clarify who owns what under such circumstances.

Today, Daniel and Don are both big guns in their field. They both have Chairs. In earlier times, though, Daniel was Don's PhD supervisor. In fact he recruited Don to work with him on a funded project. For a while they got on really well and the relationship was highly generative for both of them. However, as time went on the relationship became more rivalrous. Daniel started to assert his seniority and to claim many of Don's insights for the project. Don was incensed and tried to secure them for his PhD, even going so far as to take the case further up the university system. The rivalry had initially been contained within the project team but now it was public knowledge. Eventually it was resolved, but the deep hostilities remained and sadly spilled over into subsequent workplaces and professional relationships. People were 'recruited' either to Don's or to Daniel's team. Many colleagues did not want to take sides, as they found the whole thing distasteful.

Applying for ethics approval

If you are doing research with people (often and insultingly referred as 'human subjects') or animals you must get ethics approval from your university and possibly other research sites before you commence your research. You need to find out what the requirements are in your particular situation. In many countries and universities this should be done before submitting your grant application to the funding agency. In others, the university will only be willing to consider ethics approval once the grant is obtained. Whatever, you should already have thought about the ethical dimensions of your research when writing the research proposal, and you can find out more about this in *Getting Started on Research*.

Your university website will probably have all the details and forms on line and will also have the dates of ethics committee meetings. You may also need ethics approval from your other research sites. If you are doing research in medical settings getting ethics approval may be particularly onerous. If you haven't had to get ethics approval beforehand and you have been able to appoint a research assistant, then tracking down what you need to do in this respect is a good early job for them, as is working on early drafts of your various ethics applications. Some institutions will require you to renew your ethics approval annually – and if your project has changed you may even need to apply afresh. At the end of the project, your university may also require a final ethics report.

University ethics committees tend to be very determined and cautious, always want their instructions followed to the letter and also prefer more rather than less detail. The more you give them first up the more likely is their quick approval. They are also very conservative and don't take kindly to methodological innovation or 'out there' topics. If your project fits these descriptions put a great deal of extra care into your ethics application, carefully and convincingly laying out your legitimations and justifications.

Your publishing and dissemination plan

Authorship and attribution are among the most contentious aspects of team research. Recognise this up front and deal with it. Reach an agreement and put it in writing. The sorts of things you will need to negotiate are as follows: How the publications will be authored. Will all team members' names be on each paper? If so, in what order? How will book authorship be ordered, alphabetically or in order of contribution? How is 'contribution' to be understood? What if you do not want your name on a certain paper? Of course you have that right, but what does it do for team morale? Is having single or sub-group-authored papers the best way to go, provided they always acknowledge the project and the rest of the project team in footnotes? If so, what are your responsibilities with regard to critical feedback on others' drafts? At what point does heaps and heaps of feedback turn into at least associate authorship? Are you better-off negotiating authorship on a case-by-case basis? We have tried various methods. None is perfect and you can get stung in many unexpected ways. Don't ask us to elaborate! The main thing is to agree and to keep the lines of communication open on the topic. If the approach you agreed on does not appear to be working, talk about it and renegotiate it. Don't brood, it's an awful waste of energy.

The on-going work

Looking after your budget

You have your revised budget and you are now spending money on staff, various sorts of infrastructure and travel. Here are the questions you need answered about the university's finance practices with regard to research money:

- Can you get a credit card for your research project?
- What do you do with receipts for costs incurred outside the university? Indeed, do you have a decent system for keeping receipts?
- What can you sign off on?
- Can you, should you, keep your own accounts and records? How is this best done?
- How can you keep a check on your accounts?
- How does the university keep you informed of your expenditure?
- Can you understand the forms they send you? These are usually in totally incomprehensible codes and are organised in counter-intuitive ways.

Most early career researchers don't know the answers to these questions. However, some universities do run short training sessions on the university's finance systems and the software packages used and it very useful to go along to these so you can get up to speed quickly. If your university does not offer such things suggest to your research office that they offer them as a research training activity for new researchers. Such activity should include preparing budgets, using spreadsheets and the like. If no formal training exists, or if you have done the training and still don't understand, it may be worth going to see your finance officer and asking her or him to explain the budgeting systems to you. Not only can you ask the questions you need answered, but it will also mean that the finance officer is more likely to remember you and respond quickly to your questions in future.

You must never ever put your trust in the university to keep your records correctly and thus pass all responsibility over to it. Mistakes are always made with mysterious outgoings and incomings. You must regularly check your budgets and fix them up pronto.

Leadership and membership of research teams

The research team is central to the success of the project. It is crucial that you get your membership and leadership right. A good research team is hugely productive in many ways and is a joy to be part of. We have each been blessed on many occasions in this regard. However, we have also had some less than pleasant and productive experiences. These drag you and the research down. If you have appointed good research staff that is a good start. Research teams include the following combinations:

- The sole grant winner and:

  o Research staff.
  o Research staff and a PhD student and/or a postdoctoral appointment.
  o A project consultancy or management team invited and appointed by the grant winner or by the funder.

- A grant-winning team consisting mainly of:

  o Academics at one university or more, within one or more school, department, research centre or discipline, within one or more state or country, and research staff.
  o Research staff and a PhD student and/or a postdoctoral appointment.
  o A project consultancy or management team invited and appointed by the grant winner or by the funder.

- A grant-winning team consisting of academics and research partners from elsewhere: industry, government, the community, the profession, anywhere. This team might include any or all the above and also:

  o Research staff appointed by the partner.
  o Permanent employees of the partner whose work has been diverted to the project either part or full time.

Teams are complex and consist of many types of research identities and relationships. Team members might include very experienced researchers and novices, people with different types of research experience and with different expectations of the project's processes and outcomes.

Handy hints about team work

Being the boss. Almost inevitably teams involve some sort of formal and clear power hierarchy. Certain people are the employing researchers and others are the research workers employed on a contract and answerable to you, the boss. Being the boss does not mean being tyrannical, exploitative or a dragon of the first order. Neither does it mean becoming your staff's new best friend or their therapist, life coach or mother/father figure. It does mean taking responsibility for the work and working conditions of your employees and treating your staff with respect and care. At a minimum your role is to:

- Clearly allocate, schedule and oversee their work.
- Make sure it gets done.
- Evaluate it and assist them to improve it if necessary.
- Ensure that the conditions in which they undertake that work are conducive to working well, and are safe and healthy.
- Know the rules and procedures that govern employment in your university.

You are a *really* good boss if you do such things as:

- Give lots of feedback to your researchers about when their work is going well and how it might be improved.
- Get them to talk about how they think they are going and what might help them to work better.
- Find out if they need any additional training and organise that for them. Perhaps plan a programme for their time of employment with you.
- Keep in mind that they also have a future and consider how their involvement in the project might help them in their own career plans.
- Factor into their work any rewards that you can which will increase their enjoyment of their work and their attachment to the project.
- See your role as offering research training for your research staff and give them plenty of opportunities to build their skills through new research-related experiences.
- Help them gain new positions and/or develop their own projects as their work on yours draws to a close.

Problems!

Researcher/contract researcher relationships can get difficult if, for instance, the contract researcher is your PhD student, long-standing friend, lover, a member of your family, your daughter's best friend or whatever. Such complicated relationships are best avoided in our view. But relationships can get difficult anyway. And, of course, you may become friendly with your research staff, occasions may require that you hear their personal troubles and take into account what is going on in their personal life. But ultimately they work for you and you are together to get a job of work done under the terms of the project and their employment contract. This is the base line.

You are a problematic boss if you do not do the 'good boss' things noted above, and if you:

- Don't do what you say you will.
- Are difficult to contact and talk with.
- Keep changing your mind or their schedule.
- Are rigid and don't allow a little flexibility when it is required.
- Expect them to work above or below their job descriptions and skills.
- Expect them to work above and beyond their paid working hours.
- Don't trust them to do the right thing by you.
- Do not properly acknowledge their work, or if you claim theirs as your own, failing to include their name on the paper. Some scoundrels do this and should be shot at dawn for it. It is not on. Paying someone for their work doesn't absolve you of your moral obligation for proper acknowledgement and attribution of their contributions.
- Do not consider their career development needs and help them move on from their position as your research assistant.

You, as boss, may have problems with your research staff if they:

- Do not listen.
- Do not do as they are asked.
- Are not up to the job and more training won't get them there in the short term.
- Skive off when they are supposed to be working.
- Turn up late for meetings.
- Try to take control of the project. Some like to call this 'managing up'. In some senses your researchers will have to do it when trying

to arrange aspects of the project or trying, for instance, to organise meetings. But we are talking here about when they try to make the sorts of decisions that are rightly yours and when they will not follow your instructions to do otherwise.

- Become possessive about project data, such as field notes, regarding it as their own rather than the project team's.
- Decide what they will do at their own rather than the project's convenience.
- Expect attributions or authorships that are beyond the level of their contribution. This happens quite often, and for some clarity about who has the right to be named as an author you can read *Writing for Publication.*
- Or if you end up doing the work they are supposed to be doing or having to double-check everything they have done because you do not trust them to do it properly.

You should know that sometimes any or all such problems may arise no matter how good a boss you are. While some RAs are bliss, some are hopeless.

Dealing with problems

There are no hard-and-fast rules for dealing with these two sets of problems except that they must be nipped in the bud early and you must take the lead in doing this. The first set of problems – about being a bad boss – is particularly difficult because your RA is unlikely to give you the feedback that will enable you to be a better boss. After all, there is an imbalance of power and you are not only the boss, you are also the source of future references, job opportunities and career sponsorship. The best thing you can do is: first follow the golden 'good boss' rules listed above, second make sure the lines of communication are as open and dialogical as possible and third regularly reflect critically and ruthlessly on your own boss practices.

The second set of problems – about having a poor RA – is not easy to deal with either, particularly if you are the sort of person who finds it difficult to be frank with people or who always makes excuses for them even when they are patently behaving inappropriately or if you compulsively avoid potentially conflictual or confrontational situations. Be clear on this. Such ways of being in the world do not help you, the project or indeed the contract researcher. You must name the problem and address it as soon as you are aware of it; don't indulge in avoidance strategies, otherwise known as the strategies of the totally gutless who cannot live up to their responsibilities to the project or the employee.

Your university's 'human resources' department will be able to provide you with advice and information about processes to follow. If the situation gets so bad that you have to sack the researcher you need to know what their and your legal rights are and you will need to have followed due process. This usually requires you to have clearly laid out your performance expectations for a set period and for the assistant's performance to be evaluated at the end of that period. It also involves a number of stages, and if they do not come up to scratch at the end of them you then have grounds for dismissal. This is a big step to take and hopefully it will not come to that.

Before entering the process you may try to deal with the recalcitrant staff member informally. There are a number of tactics you could try:

- Call a meeting and let the person know that you have concerns about their work and that you want to talk to them about the problem and how to resolve it quickly and without rancour.
- List your concerns and email your list to your researcher. Invite them to come to the meeting with an explanation and also with a set of propositions about how they might get up to speed.
- In the meeting first go though your concerns. Give them the chance to go though their responses to your concerns and to lay out any of their own. Quietly but firmly get them to agree that they must lift their game. (And, if you need to lift yours, then agree to do that too but do not take any blame where it is not warranted.) Go through their proposed ways of doing this. Share some of your own and let them know how you will monitor their work. Set out a time period for the first stage of this monitoring and let them know that if they are not up to speed, your next step is the formal university process.
- You must keep good, written records of all of this.

Louise was really rushed to appoint a research assistant on a new project of the 'starting Monday' variety. Jim worked down the corridor, seemed friendly and capable and had just finished his contract on another project. She got chatting to him at the photocopier ▶

▶ and before she knew it she was offering him the job – starting immediately. She did not have a chance to contact his previous employer until a few weeks into the project, at which time she learnt that he had been unsatisfactory and had actually been under a process of formal review. Louise had always been rather unimpressed with the previous employer and anyway thought that her superior people skills would ensure that Jim got up speed. Further, she had no time to follow though with the HR people to find out exactly what had happened and what it might mean for her work with Jim. As time went on she found that indeed Jim was below par and that he spent lots of time and effort trying to hide the fact. He took twice as long to do things as was reasonable but got defensive when she tried to 'intervene'. Meanwhile she found that she was regularly having to check his work, as she could never be sure that it would be done properly. When she had finally had enough and decided to institute a process of review herself, she found that she did not know how to go about it. By the time she found out, it became clear to her that she had no decent evidence of his poor work history because she herself had in fact covered over the trail. When she told him she intended nonetheless to institute proceedings, he was furious and complained about her to the union and senior staff. All this took huge amounts of time away from the project but she did not let the funder know of the problems she was having. Eventually a 'deliverable' was due that she could not deliver. The funder charged her a penalty from the next round of money she was due to get. When she protested, the funder pointed to the contract, which neither she nor the university solicitor had read before she signed it. She had no choice but to keep Jim on for the remainder of the project and to fund, out of another consultancy budget line, someone else to do his work.

Being a member of a collegial academic team

What of relationships within a project team consisting mainly of experienced or fledgling academics, including project PhD students and postdoctoral fellows (postdocs)? These need care too, especially when there are big differences of power and status.

Formal and informal lines of responsibility, authority and accountability

With the PhD students and the postdocs on your team it is likely you will also be their boss in that they were invited on to your project and thus work to you – although, as noted earlier, ownership of ideas and authorship of publications may be an issue. In such cases many of the points we made about being a good and very good boss apply. There may be chief and partner investigators on the team. Again it is clear that the responsibility for the project and the lines of authority within it are with the CIs. Also, if there is, or you are, a project director then the buck stops with them/you.

If you are all named on the project bid as CIs then it is open slather even if some team members are more junior than others. There are few guidelines even though this is the most common form of research practice. In such circumstances you would be well advised to attend to the following matters and to invent your own rules for the project no matter whether it is a long one or a short one.

Very early in the project negotiate *roles and responsibilities* and do up a responsibility matrix. We give an example of such a matrix in Table 5. You need to make sure that responsibilities are distributed equally and that no-one gets more to do than the others and that no-one gets more of the cream or the crap jobs than do others. However, too much democracy can be as problematic as too little. It is smart to make use of the particular skills people have. So, for instance, if one of the team is brilliant at statistics and the rest mediocre, it makes sense and is of overall benefit to the project if the stats person plays to their strengths. This may mean you do more menial things at some stages of the project. So what! There will be swings and roundabouts. On other occasions you may be doing the higher-order stuff while she is making the coffee. In other words, don't be too precious or too short-term in your thinking about team democracy. View project work in the whole and take things in the round. That said, more senior researchers have a responsibility to more junior colleagues to make sure that they are getting what they need out of a project and aren't being exploited by their ethically challenged colleagues and that they are not exploiting themselves. And the load will also be distributed according to role and level of responsibility.

TABLE 5   A responsibility matrix

Name	Role	Budget/ money	Talking to funder	Literature review and fieldwork	Data analysis	Writing
Jamila	Chief investigator	✓	✓	10%	Supervisory Keeping an overview	Lead role
Peter	Partner investigator			10%	Quantitative data	Quantitative aspects
Anne	Research associate			50% (and to help Ilan). Setting up access to research sites	Qualitative data	Support Jamila and Peter
Ilan	Part-time research assistant PT doctoral student			30% with special attention to the literature review	Support to Peter and Anne	

Ethical practice in research teams

Not all research bosses or general members of a research team are highly reflexive about their own practices and some have no clue. Sadly, also, some contract researchers or junior members of research teams do not even know when they are getting ripped off. You are being exploited if:

- You wrote or contributed significantly to the conceptualisation of the bid but you are not a co-applicant (unless it is your job specifically to be developing bids with and in support of other people).
- You are employed fractionally but are working much more than that.
- You are employed as a research assistant but you are doing the work of a more senior research associate.
- Your work on a project is not appropriately recognised or acknowledged, e.g. you did a substantial amount of analysis of quantitative data but that's not acknowledged.
- Someone else uses your ideas without acknowledgement.

When there is a project team consisting of a number of academics it is sometimes not made clear to the research support staff what the *lines of authority and accountability* are. How should they work to a team? How can you avoid giving them conflicting directives? It is beneficial all round if there are clear lines of accountability: who should they go to first, who should they go to for what? In the early stages of the project the academics on the team would be well advised to sort this out and to discuss together what it means to be good and very good bosses and then for the rest of the project to monitor their progress on it, perhaps by including it as an item at your regular meetings.

Regular and open communication

Such communication among the project team is crucial. It is useful at the start to develop a detailed calendar of meetings for a semester and also to plan some key dates for the year. Team meetings need to take place quite frequently so that you don't lose track of what is happening in the project. The more complex the work, the more frequently they need to be held. In addition to regular meetings of the whole team (if it consists of more than one main researcher with assistance), there need to be more frequent regular meetings between any contract researchers and the researcher they are working with. Such meetings may need to take place as often as once a week or once a fortnight – fieldwork permitting. Your more regular meetings will involve lots of routine project management activities and of necessity will include regular budget updates but should also include progress reports and recurring discussions of the research itself, perhaps based on the progress reports. You might also have your research assistant do a regular email communication bulletin. Set these dates early and in stone. Under no circumstances keep altering them because others want you to. You research must take high priority. Try to include some project team retreats so that you can go away together and enjoy some serious project thinking time. You might use this time to discuss your data or your reading or to workshop your papers.

Dealing with different working styles

Among team members working styles vary. Some members may need huge lead times, for instance, while others may work best under the pressure of fierce deadlines. Try to get to know the different ways of working among team members and accommodate them in your plans. On the other hand, though, because it is a team, you may need to modify your ways in order to progress the team's plans. It's a fine line, but being aware of the issues is a good start.

Time-lines

Your time-lines were produced as part of the project application and revised in line with the reduced budget. They may also need to be revised owing to other things that delay you: achieving ethics approval or getting access to the field, for instance. Clearly your time-line is a moving feast to some extent but it should not be too movable or you will not complete the project on time and it will haunt you while you are trying to do later projects. If some things delay you in one aspect of the project, do other project-related work. This might include such activities as your reading on theory or methods, updating the literature review, working though some thorny conceptual problems or designing research instruments. *There is no such thing as down time on research projects.*

Don't get interrupted by anything outside the project

If you have taken our advice about planning the rest of your teaching and admin work alongside your research, you have no excuses. But some people lack self-discipline. In a highly Pavlovian manner, they respond to every stimulus out there. It is one thing to respond to a reasonable request from your head of school, say, for you to take on some unexpected new activity above and beyond what you knew to expect when you planned your research project's timetable. It is entirely another for you to rush off to everything that looks interesting at the expense of the project which is supposed to be one of your primary responsibilities. If you do this it shows little respect for your research team and also of course drives them crazy. 'No' must be in your vocabulary, and remember, opportunities come along all the time; to miss one is not to miss them all for ever.

Dissemination activities

You should try to keep to your publishing plan but it should be sufficiently flexible to admit out-of-left-field opportunities. However you organise authorship, you should certainly do conference symposia and other public fora together as well as separately. This is vital for the visibility of the project as a whole and it offers you opportunities to collectively test out your ideas in public and to get feedback. It has other benefits, not the least being that you get to go away together and have fun. More invitations to present again on the project are among the usual benefits, unless of course your symposium goes down like a lead balloon. If that happens at least you are there to support each other and can go off together and do group therapeutic activity. We have found that if the papers are badly received the fact itself can provoke some quite generative discussions both at the conference and later. So don't be too gloomy about it. You should make sure you encourage each other to turn conference presentations into papers for peer-refereed journals. Don't make the common mistake of too many conference presentations and not enough publications.

Your dissemination plan may also include developing (and regularly updating!) your website, regular media releases, workshops for industry, promo talks to potential users, talk-back radio and the like. Keep a list of journalists you have found helpful and competent and use them regularly. You do not have to wait till you have conclusive findings; work in progress material is always of interest. Your dissemination plan may also include conferences or workshops that you organise yourselves. These might be highly specialised, by invitation and include only academics in your field. Or they may be designed to speak to policy makers or practitioners and be open to all comers, or specified cohorts. In allocating dissemination responsibilities you might put certain members in charge of overseeing such activities and making sure they happen. It is too easy to let such things slip to the bottom of the list. All research projects should have some sort of *public profile* and you have to build it. In doing so you may take advice from your university's media and PR people. Often the media people are looking for copy and will run stories for you. You should also make sure you and your project are listed on the university's register of expertise or the equivalent.

Acknowledgement

Acknowledging each other's contribution to the work of the team is important. But how does the team recognise and deal with the big ideas of individuals? If someone has had an idea that you can clearly identify as having influenced your thinking it must be acknowledged. However, often in project teams such big ideas are a result of the synergies among the group and it is hard to pin them down to one individual or moment. We thus urge you not to be too precious about this with regard to ideas you think are yours. They may have arisen from the springboard of the group and you may not be acknowledging it sufficiently. On the other hand breakthough thoughts or compelling or evocative new concepts may well deserve to be acknowledged. A little generosity goes a long way. And remember that you need to go on acknowledging the collaboration of your team long after the actual project has ended, whenever you use data collected during the project or the big ideas from it.

Different opportunities among the team

Dealing with these differences is crucial. In many teams there are people who get more invitations than others to strut their stuff at conferences, in print or to the media. If you are such a person try to share some of the opportunities with other members of the team. If you don't, public perceptions of the project will be skewed towards you and also, eventually, there will be undercurrents of resentment within the project team. On the other hand, if you are not one of these people it does you no good to get resentful or envious. Take the opportunities that are available to you to get out and about even if they do not arise from invitations. Volunteer papers, submit proposals for symposia, let people know who you are and of your availability to talk on the project. All such things will enhance your profile in regard to the project and also the project itself – which is the main game, is it not?

Slackers and what to do about them

What do you do if some team members do not share the load equally? One always hopes that if one pulls one's own weight others will pull theirs. But sadly this is not always the case. Sometimes people fall in a heap for personal and entirely understandable reasons, and you can usually live with that for a while as they will eventually come out of it, hopefully sooner rather than later. If it goes on for too long you do need to deal with it, because maybe they can't. However, some people are just plain lazy and are happy for others to do their leg work, and yet others are too busy doing other things to attend properly to the project. It is very hard to sort out such situations. Yet failure to do so can lead to serious rifts within the team. If you have done many of the things we suggest above you may minimise the problem but some people have very thick skins.

Our view is that you should, as always, try to nip the problem in the bud and put the issue up front and on the agenda of meetings. Sometimes all your best efforts have no effect. What do you do then? We think you should cut your losses and count them out. It is not appropriate for them to get credit where credit is not due – and credit for work on your project which they are not actually doing might include some significant benefits to them, such as a reduced work load, access to project money, recognition with regard to project outcomes and so on. That would be plain unfair. You may want to formally negotiate their departure from the project and have funding authorities and the university record the fact. Such a step is serious, and even the threat of it may get them moving. If you do not wish to go that far then we suggest you rewrite the rules the project has negotiated in such a way as to ensure that the person is excluded from project benefits. Certainly their name should not go on any publications or acknowledgements. If, however, they made a big contribution in the early stages of the project and fell by the wayside later, you must acknowledge their early contribution.

Falling out with members of the team

This is not uncommon and neither is it the end of the world, even though it hurts. This can happen at any stage of the project and over any of its activities. Rightly or wrongly, people may feel marginalised in the team or undervalued, they may feel their ideas are neglected, that they carry too much of the load or that some people get more credit than they do. There may be genuine theoretical, methodological or political differences in the team that cannot be reconciled, or totally incompatible working styles. You do need to be alert to the falling-out warning signs in yourself and in others. You might, for example, find yourself constantly anxious or negative about the project, or that after meetings or field trips you come away with feelings of irritability, hostility or disappointment with regard to your co-researchers, or you might feel jealous each time they speak because they are so articulate in comparison with your view of yourself or they get the attention you crave or feel you deserve. All this might lead you to withdraw from them or to make bitchy remarks behind their backs or whatever. In others, these warning signs might include negative body language, withdrawal, hostile, defensive, sarcastic or disruptive behaviour in meetings, a tense and fraught aura when the team is together, the formation of team sub-sets who go their own way or who respond negatively to everything that others do.

How do you deal with such things? You probably need to develop some 'emotional literacy' with regard to your own negative feelings and behaviours. They may arise because you are tired and overworked, because other things are going badly in your life or because you are insecure or paranoid. It is not fair on your co-researchers to project it all on to them. So you do have to get a grip; try to deal with the root causes, get counselling if it will help. On the other hand there may be good reasons for your negative mind set, although if you are paranoid you will be unable to distinguish between these good reasons and your paranoid fantasies. The team may indeed not be working as well as it might. This is the point at which you have to speak up, without dumping on your colleagues, let people know how you feel and ask how the group might collectively improve the situation. This may work; it may not. Some things are not resolvable. Having tried your best you may just have to work and live the project out, or cut your losses and get out if you can do so without too much damage to your reputation or the team. You must then resolve not to work with certain people again.

Four overarching principles apply to the personal dynamics of working in research teams:

- Be very careful who you get into bed with.
- If you are going to err, it's better to err on the side of generosity. There is no place in research for the small-minded or the mean spirited.
- Don't take everything too much to heart – save your angst for the big things that really matter. There is no place in research for the over-sensitive ego.

- If you get seriously, badly, deeply stung don't work with those people again but also don't go around publicly ruining their reputations. They will do that by themselves – eventually, hopefully.

Everybody (or nearly everybody) has a *dream team* in their head. In this team, the ideas would flow, the work would go smoothly, everyone would agree, stimulate and support everyone else all the time, no-one would suffer any angst over the project, everything would run to time and the outputs would be outstanding. Unfortunately, such a dream team doesn't exist. In practice, as with all other relationships, teams need to be worked at. You should no more expect to be part of a perfect team than you expect to have a perfect relationship at all times with your mother, lover or friends. What matters is that the team is good enough and that members of it are prepared to work at making things work.

Relationships between the team and the funder

These are on-going. They don't end once you have the money in your hot little hand (the university's account, actually). All sorts of to-ing and fro-ing will be required, some of which we have already mentioned and is to do with regular reporting and delivery requirements and which may involve dealing with a management team. However, other things may arise as the project proceeds. It is helpful to know that funders often have one person who is your contact and whom you should cultivate. Being on the good side of this person can be very handy at times. Your project might be wise to specify the team member who will be in regular touch with the funder. If there's someone in the team who is particularly adept at that sort of thing, then let him or her deal with it, although you may want to learn some skills from them for future application in different projects. You should always let the funder know if you are seriously behind, or having major difficulties, or have to make significant changes. This is not just a courtesy, it is a necessity. You need to cover yourself and have their agreement to such changes (preferably in writing if need be). But you may also be able to get some help and advice from them with regard to the trouble you are having. The funder is not an ogre, at least not often, and they want to get the project done, and done well, as much as you do. So don't put your funder in an awkward position, ever. It may come back to bite you. Good relationships are always of benefit, personally and professionally. If you are working in a sensitive area and you have some trouble brewing (e.g. hostile journalists phoning you) then make sure you contact the funder, who may have better resources and press officers to deal with it than you have at your disposal. Discuss how best to address the issues.

While funders are not ogres, they can also be pretty damn demanding and can try to squeeze more work out of you than you have been paid for. This may happen at the end of the project in negotiating the final product, or after the project is over they may want you to be involved in a raft of dissemination activities above and beyond those you agreed to. If so, you naturally expect to be paid. Your time requires their money. Don't be a sucker and don't forever give your time for free. They will not respect you in the morning.

Being a member of a team that includes industry partners or government

Many of the things we said above about research teams apply here, but there are some additional matters to consider. These vary for many reasons, including how the funding has been gained. You and your industry partner may have joined forces to gain money from a third party, or perhaps industry has provided the money and contracted you to do the work along with its research staff. There are other options we could list but the point is that the method of funding will determine the power relations within the team and the main pressures on the team. If industry funded you or if it has put more resources into the project than you then it holds most of the aces.

You may find that you and your industry partner have somewhat different values and cultures. Of course you must not assume significant differences exist or go into the research with your mind full of stereotypes – but you may, nonetheless, find such differences and you have to work to try to bridge them. This does not mean that you have to subordinate your culture to theirs, or they theirs to yours. But it probably does mean acknowledging that such differences exist and considering where they advantage the project and where they get in the way. Keep in mind that differences can be very generative and exciting, so don't be afraid of them or dig your heels in unnecessarily.

You will be able to iron out any potentially debilitating differences in the probably protracted process of putting the grant application together – a process that requires both you and your partners to compromise. Such differences may have to do with the research focus or styles or IP and publishing and you may well have found each other's processes annoying. Obviously you would not be proceeding with the research had you not been able to resolve those differences – but that may only have been on the surface and they may simmer for some time. As always, there are no hard-and-fast rules about how to deal with them. The best advice we can offer is to do so early and in as dialogical a manner as is possible.

Winding up, gearing up?

All good things come to an end (and so, thankfully, do the less good). But when is the project finished? Apart from deadlines bearing down on you, there is also the matter of the money running out – and, inevitably, you've so much more that you could still do in relation to the project. Hopefully by this point you will have fulfilled all your promises. You have now:

- Let all your research staff go after due farewells and assistance with future employment.
- Offered your final acknowledgements to participants and undertaken any acts of reciprocity that you deemed necessary and that they wanted.
- Written the final reports.
- Put out the requisite publications, which are being well reviewed and cited.
- Had the impact you hoped.
- Run your budget dry but not overspent it.
- Carefully archived all the material on CDs and in archive boxes or files.

Is that all there is? Is it the end? Well, no, not if you are a career researcher. This is the start of another project. Where you have left off is a place to begin again.

3 Thinking through Networks

In this chapter we help you think through three of the more complex issues that arise in relation to networking. You need to address working ethically, who owns the fruits of networked labour and, finally, planning your own networking. These topics are linked in the sense that if you don't pay careful attention to them, they may well come back and bite you.

Ethical networking/networking ethics

Because of the complex relationships implied, networking activities can generate a lot of ethical dilemmas and challenges for academics. Here are some examples of what we mean:

- You have agreed to meet somebody at a conference at their request. It is not a meeting you are particularly looking forward to and you're unsure what's in it for you. Subsequently you get an invitation, from someone who you really want to meet, at exactly the same time. What do you do?
- You are doing academic research that necessitates networking with people in a government department that is a major stakeholder in your work. The officials in the department offer you a significant consultancy fee (which would be yours to keep personally) if you do some work for them that will assist the government's policy objectives. The trouble is that you disagree on moral grounds with those policies. You know that the government will be trading on your research reputation in using your work. Such situations require a delicate balancing act between staying true to your own moral beliefs and ethical values, whilst at the same time not offending your stakeholders.

- You have done some research that has caught the attention of the media. A journalist wants to run a story about your work, but is quite insistent that you name the organisations that were respondents in your research. This would breach the assurances of confidentiality that you gave to the organisations. Even so, you do want the media to cover your research.

Academics are, or should be, accustomed to considering the ethical dimensions of research work. Indeed, universities often have procedures, committees or guidelines to instil, enforce or regulate ethical practice in research. Networking presents its own significant and substantial ethical issues, but these are rarely discussed and are seldom the subject of any formal procedures. The absence of informal discussion or formal governance means that it is imperative to keep your ethical antennae extended.

Much of what we mean by ethical networking is implicit in what we've already said about reciprocity. That is, you should not be purely instrumental or exploitative and must be sensitive to power relations. Faustian bargains are never a good idea, and you should not use your networks to improper personal or professional advantage.

John is a professor who does a great deal of consultancy for the New Zealand government. One of his part-time doctoral students is a senior civil servant who, on occasion, issues consultancy contracts. John accepted such a lucrative contract from this student. He presented it to his university without disclosing that the person responsible for letting the contract was, in fact, a student of the university and closely connected with him. Furthermore, he represented the work to be done as 'research'. In fact the government had placed stringent conditions in the contract, preventing the team involved from publishing the results of the work. He did not recognise that his unethical actions placed his student, his university and himself in jeopardy and had the potential to prejudice future stakeholder networker relations between his university and this government department.

Each type of network that we identified earlier – academic, stakeholder and dissemination – has a particular set of ethical issues associated with it. We will deal with each in turn.

In networking with other academics, you should try and build the following sorts of responses and behaviours into your work:

- Attribute ideas to their rightful source and don't wrongly claim them as your own. '
- Ensure that you do not use your power to exclude or discriminate against people.
- Act kindly towards people and help them, especially when they are junior to you or in a vulnerable position.
- Be honest when someone who is applying for a job or a grant asks you to act as a referee. If your reference will be negative, to a greater or lesser extent, you should give the person an opportunity to find someone more positive.
- Be generous and fair in providing feedback to help people improve their work, whether as an anonymous peer reviewer or as a known colleague.
- Be careful, especially in public forums, to behave respectfully towards your colleagues, even when engaging with their work critically. In the case of inexperienced researchers, you need to be particularly sensitive as to how you couch your responses.

Miriam does a lot of refereeing for a journal that actively seeks to promote critical and well theorised research. The US editor of this journal sees one of his editorial roles as being to develop and bring on researchers in his field who are often quite isolated within their own institutions. When he receives papers, which are often clearly weak, from such isolated researchers he does not reject them out of hand as many editors would do. Instead, he sends them out to carefully selected reviewers, requesting them to give careful and detailed guidance to the author on how to make the paper publishable. Before sending her comments back, Miriam always puts her review on one side for a couple of days and then rereads it prior to despatch, asking herself the question 'How would I feel if I got these comments on one of my own papers?'

In networking with stakeholders, you need to think about a different range of considerations.

- Choose who you get into bed with, in a network sense, carefully. You will have to make individual decisions and choices about who constitutes an ethically acceptable partner for you, your colleagues and your institution.
- Do not allow your work or your reputation to be used by your stakeholder network partners in inappropriate ways.
- Be sensitive to the employment positions of people in non-academic organisations with whom you are networking. You need to understand and take account of the pressures and constraints that they operate under. This means not disclosing information given to you in confidence and not 'dropping them in it' with their colleagues or bosses.

Dissemination networks involve ethical considerations that are different again.

- You must try to ensure that media coverage of your research does not compromise any individual, group or institution. This goes beyond questions of the anonymity of individual respondents to include situations where your findings might fuel pejorative public stereotypes of certain groups of people.
- Although most media people are highly professional with good ethical practices of their own, some may attempt to distort or be highly selective with your research findings.
- Do unto others as you would be done by. Exercise sound academic judgement and be fair when you are asked to review books or papers for publication. That is, do not use your power, position or voice unfairly. It is inappropriate to use such opportunities to make personal attacks on individuals. Negative reviews, even more than positive ones, must be very carefully framed and evidenced.
- Ensure that, when you author government or other 'official' reports, you do not give in to any pressure to distort what you say or the recommendations that you make. This can be tough and may require sustained negotiation and possibly even institutional support.
- Give credit where credit is due in the authorship of any reports or other dissemination. Named authors could well include people in stakeholder organisations who have helped substantially in the

research process. However, you should resist including the names of people who have made no real contribution to the work (or the stakeholders who simply 'managed' the work) in the list of authors.

Later in this book we identify some specific strategies to address these issues.

Laura was part of a team researching the control of drug use by students in schools. Schools were understandably nervous about giving access for such research, as they did not want any dirty linen washed in public. The team negotiated a good confidentiality policy with the participating schools, which were part of the stakeholder network. Subsequently, a TV company approached the researchers and said that they wanted to make a serious documentary and requested the team to negotiate access to the schools for them. This had the potential to be a good dissemination opportunity for the researchers. However, they turned it down because they were aware that the media exposure could have had very negative consequences for the schools involved.

Intellectual property rights

In knowledge economies, knowledge is a tradable commodity. This means that participants in such an economy need to pay attention to who owns and controls the knowledge that is traded. As knowledge economies have grown, people have increasingly sought to assert their legal rights over knowledge. Such 'knowledge' is usually called 'intellectual property' (IP) and is subject to three main property rights: patents (or know-how on how to do things), designs (what things could/should look like) and copyright (the use and publication of words, images, text, sounds, etc.). In the arts, social sciences and humanities the most important form of IP is copyright. You can find out more about this in *Writing for Publication*.

Because universities see themselves as major players in the knowledge economy, they are increasingly paying a lot of attention to these issues. This means that you can't avoid them either. Whether what you produce in the form of IP belongs to you or to your university will depend upon your contract of employment, and you should familiarise yourself with what that contract says. Generally, universities now claim ownership of everything you produce in the execution of your contractual duties. However, most allow you to keep the copyright in written works. This really isn't generosity; it's because academic publications usually make so little money. Remember that the law is different in each country, so as well as checking your contract, it would be useful to check what the law is in the place where you work. Here we deal with those aspects of IP that arise specifically with regard to networks and partnerships.

Any collaborative teaching or research work that involves academic or stakeholder networks may give rise to three intellectual property rights (IPR) issues: (1) *Research materials*: who owns and/or controls the materials used in or created by the research process? (2) *Publications*: who has the right to be known as the author of any material and who has the right to publish such materials or software? (3) *Teaching materials*: when you develop teaching materials, who can claim them as their IP? We will discuss each of these in turn.

Research materials

There are two sorts of material here. One is material that belongs to, or access to which is controlled by, someone other than the researcher(s). The other is material that is created by the researcher(s). If research involves the use of material where the IP belongs to someone else, you will need to be very careful to ensure that any necessary permissions are obtained for its use and for any subsequent publications. For instance, if you are a historian using someone's books and papers from a private archive, you will need to make up-front arrangements about the use of and quotations from them and make sure that you stick faithfully to them.

Second, the research process will invariably involve the creation of a whole host of intellectual products. These will include research instruments (e.g. interview schedules, questionnaires and so on), data (for example, survey results, transcripts, fieldwork notes) and all kinds of project documentation, from the proposal itself to minutes of meetings, sketches, diagrams, research notebooks and so on.

If you are working with others in an academic network, you need to make very explicit agreements about the ownership of such materials and how they may be used. However, if you simply share an idea or set of ideas with other members of the team without recording this idea anywhere, then you cannot claim economic IPR over these ideas, though you may have a moral right to attribution (see *Writing for Publication* for definitions of these terms). Ultimately, your best protection is to have good, open relations with your colleagues and to discuss these important issues with them before they become a crisis or a bone of contention.

Samantha, from the USA, was working with academics from a number of other institutions on a major research project that generated a lot of data, including interview transcripts. While the project was in process, all team members shared all the data generated. Publications arising directly from the project listed all the team members as authors. They agreed that when the project was wound up, any of them could continue to use their pooled data. They further agreed that subsequent publications would always include an acknowledgement of the source of the data and list the project team. However, authorship would be confined to those people who had actually worked on that particular publication.

Sometimes, on funded projects, the data created will remain the property of the people who gave you the money to do the research. This can be very problematic and interfere with your academic freedom. If somebody else is going to own the data that your project creates, you need to make absolutely sure that you are clear about what you are getting into and what you are letting go of, and carefully negotiate any use rights that you may want.

Publications

There are two IP aspects here, whether you are working with academic or stakeholder networks. First, who gets named as an author? Second, who has the right to control the contents of the publication and even whether it is published or not?

We deal with the question of authorship at length in *Writing for Publication*. But remember that, with few exceptions, all genuine authors of a text have a moral right of attribution – that is, they have a right to be known and recognised as author. If you are writing in the context of an academic or stakeholder network, you may come under pressure to include people as authors who did not contribute in a significant way to the publication. Such pressure may come from more senior academic colleagues, the funding organisation or people whose contribution to the project was essentially clerical – such as photocopying or fetching books from the library. Further pressure can come from people who are technically part of the team but actually don't do any work on the project and none of the writing. As Stavros's story, below, shows, occasionally people have the cheek to take over the work that you have generated.

Stavros had organised a symposium at a major international research conference. He was a doctoral student but had brought together some of the best-known researchers in his field. Furthermore, he had identified the theme, had written the proposal to be refereed and generally done all the conceptual and organisational work associated with putting it together and making it happen.

The symposium was a runaway success, generating considerable interest from audience and publishers alike. When Stavros returned to Greece, he found an email from two of the stellar symposium participants inviting him to contribute a chapter to the edited collection that they planned to publish arising from the symposium. Stavros's initial reaction was delight at being invited to contribute a chapter to a book edited by two of the superstars in his field. He excitedly contacted his supervisor to tell her about this *coup*.

Her reaction was very different. She said, 'Oh, please! The entire symposium was your idea and your work, Stavros. I suggest you write to these people pointing this out and indicate your willingness to share editorship with them.' Stavros took his supervisor's advice and together they crafted a polite but firm email pointing out that he had created the symposium and that his supervisor had suggested that he might invite them to join him in editing a book. Stavros was eventually able to negotiate that he became the first named editor of the book, recognising the benefits of editing a collection in such illustrious company. Ultimately the network was strengthened as a result of Stavros's tactful but assertive response.

If you are going to do a specific piece of work that involves funding from, or working with, stakeholder organisations, then you need to clarify the ground rules around publications from the outset. Government departments, especially where sensitive policy matters are concerned, and corporations, where there might be matters of commercial secrecy, will require sensitive but assertive handling in this regard. You have to respect any legitimate needs of these stakeholders and, conversely, they have to be encouraged to appreciate the imperatives on you both to adhere to rigorous academic standards and to publish your work. All kinds of complications can arise if you think you will be able to publish and turn out not to be, as Birgit's story shows.

Birgit and some colleagues from another university were commissioned by a government agency to undertake a major research project and to produce a report for government. Birgit and her colleagues were concerned to ensure that they were able to publish from the project in academic journals and to give papers at academic conferences. They therefore asked the university solicitors at both universities to negotiate with the agency to secure that end.

The government acceded to their request, but only on condition that no such publications were produced until six months after the publication of the official report. In the event, the government held up publication of the report for some considerable time after it had been submitted, delaying for considerably longer than might reasonably have been expected.

This left the researchers in a very difficult position. They had submitted an abstract for a conference symposium, thinking that their report would have been published at least six months before the date when they would give their paper. In fact, it was eventually published just three weeks before the conference began. Fortunately, because of their carefully built networks, they were able to negotiate the funder's permission to give the conference paper.

You may feel uncomfortable about raising such issues at the start of a project, but it is essential to do so, diplomatically but assertively. One of the ways in which such discussions and any subsequent renegotiations can be made easier is by having built good contacts and relationships with the relevant individuals in the stakeholder organisation, as Birgit's story shows.

Teaching materials

Universities now frequently seek to maximise their income stream by 'selling' courses, either by registering students or by franchising course materials. If you are producing such materials you need to know that the university may claim them as its own IP. What many universities have failed to understand is that teaching materials are often the product of a genuine academic collegial networking process. Academics frequently swap materials with promiscuous abandon and think such promiscuity is laudable for obvious reasons. It's creative, synergistic, efficient, economical of time and effort and therefore just plain good sense. So, claiming IPR in such circumstances is a highly problematic thing to do, as such claims fail to recognise the provenance of the material. They also fail to recognise the ways in which academics regularly network and the limitations of the possibility of commodifying knowledge.

Shamila and Naoko got to know each other as doctoral students and shared a common interest in postcolonial theory and its application to media studies. As doctoral students in the same university they developed a course in postcoloniality and the media, which they taught together. Since graduating and taking up employment in universities in their home countries, they have both introduced this course and continued to share by email the ways they have developed it. They share lecture notes, lesson plans, new ideas about readings and examples, reflections on how particular sessions went and so on. It is difficult to tell which person invented which bits of their courses. However, each of their universities now wishes to claim IPR in Shamila and Naoko's joint work and to franchise them. In this instance, networking about teaching has become, on the one hand, a very generative and productive process and on the other very problematic. Whose intellectual property is it?

Planning networking

It can be inferred from what we have said thus far that the smart networker sees networking as more of an extension of their personality

TABLE 1 *Planning networks.* Judy is a new lecturer in social geography. She has recently completed her PhD and is now setting about the task of building on the relatively limited, mainly academic networks built up during her time as a doctoral student. She does, however, have some innovative research in the field of the geographies of social exclusion. Here is her plan. As we have said, these three sorts of networks shade into each other, and this is evident from Judy's plan

Year	Academic networks	Stakeholder networks	Dissemination networks
1	Attend and give papers at two conferences, one in this country and one abroad, funded by the university Contact my PhD examiner (as he loved my thesis) and ask if he minds being named as a referee for my book proposal Remain on the social geography e-list and take part in discussions Talk to Robyn [PhD supervisor] about whether we could do a joint grant application towards the end of the year and building on my PhD work	Ask my PhD supervisor to introduce me to her contacts in relevant government Ministries Write a lay person's brief report on my PhD and send it to selected relevant Ministries and voluntary sector, explaining briefly what my future research plans are Contact selected stakeholders who might support my next project and talk them through it	Finish the three papers in progress drawn from my PhD and send them off – aim to do one per term this year Complete my book proposal (drafted already when preparing for the examination of my thesis) Use the lay person's brief report as the basis of a short article in a suitable practitioners' journal
2	Organise a panel at the national conference of social geographers Finalise and submit grant application together with Robyn Attend specialist conference on social exclusion being held in Durban and give paper there	Keep in touch with stakeholders in project work regarding the funding application. See if they will consider joint funding. If application is successful, will need to liaise with them pretty swiftly See if I can get someone from the Ministry to participate in my conference panel from a policy perspective	Write up and submit for publication the two papers given at conferences last year. Work on the book (hopefully with a contract)
3	Together with other members of my panel, put together a proposal for an edited collection of the papers. Decide which conferences to attend – one here and one abroad if possible. With colleagues here, offer to organise the next but one social geography conference at this university	If the project is funded, will need to draw stakeholders into the research, both as informants and a couple on the project advisory committee	Finish the book Write up and submit papers from last year's conferences

than just a serendipitous process. Whilst the right kind of personal approach is necessary, it is not sufficient to make you a successful networker. We think it is also helpful for people to include networking in their academic planning. One of the major benefits is that it will help you to ensure that your networking is integrated with your research and teaching plans, supporting them in a timely manner. The danger of not planning is that simply responding opportunistically may leave you running to catch up with events and that you may not be able to do what you would like (for example, in setting up research sites) if you haven't got the relevant networks in place in advance.

In *Winning and Managing Research Funding* we encourage you to develop a three-year plan with regard to your researcher identity. You may like to remind yourself of the template and then draw up a plan like the one in Table 1 that addresses each of the three types of network. Whilst trying to avoid the risk of being totally instrumental, address the question 'Which links in which networks will help me to achieve the outcomes I want?' It would be sensible to develop networks across the range. You might also find it handy to develop a list of first contact points. Ultimately you need to get a solid understanding of the stakeholder groups.

This chapter has alerted you to three areas that need your close attention. We'll now go on in Chapters 3, 4 and 5 respectively to look at the three main types of network that we have identified for you: academic, stakeholder and dissemination.